elemental healing

elemental healing

A 5-Element Path for Ancestor Connection,
Balanced Energy, and an Aligned Life

by camellia lee

STERLING ETHOS

New York

STERLING ETHOS
New York

STERLING ETHOS and the distinctive Sterling Ethos logo are registered trademarks
of Sterling Publishing Co., Inc.

Text © 2023 Camellia Lee

ISBN 978-1-4549-4864-3
ISBN 978-1-4549-4865-0 (e-book)

Library of Congress Control Number: 2022951342

For information about custom editions, special sales, and premium purchases,
please contact specialsales@unionsquareandco.com.

Printed in India

2 4 6 8 10 9 7 5 3 1

unionsquareandco.com

Cover design by Elizabeth Mihaltse Lindy
Interior design by Rich Hazelton

Image credits appear on p. 196

For my ancestors and for all cycle-breakers healing their lineages.

CONTENTS

Part Four. Water: Ancestral Inventory

Part Five. Wood: Love in Action

INTRODUCTION

Descending the spiral staircase of DNA in my cells, I emerge in the ancestral shrine. Crimson tablets hand-painted with gold line the walls like dragon scales, shimmering in candlelight. I kneel on the cushion spattered with incense dust, cradling a plate with carefully stacked oranges. After first touching it to my head, I place the pyramid of fruit before an incense urn. The air is heavy with whispered prayers. Bowing my head to the floor three times, I silently say my name, birthday, and address so that my blessings know where to find me. Mantras softly murmur in my ears, lulling the sleeping dead into a restorative rest.

Shang dynasty archaeological evidence indicates that this practice is nothing new. Three thousand years ago, ancient Chinese society prioritized relationships with the emperor's ancestors above all else. Bronze relics from that era are largely ceremonial, and the few weapons appear to be ritual items. Written records mostly chronicle divination, not trade.

When I center lineage work, I continue a pattern written in my nuclei, practices that countless relatives have continued across oceans and language barriers. This book is a beam of light from my heart, radiating through the prism of my paternal cultural inheritance. I am writing from the specificity of my own experience because that is what I know, but my heart's light speaks the same language as yours.

In Daoism, the Undifferentiated Origin 無極 is the original state of limitless nondistinction. From the Origin arise Yin and Yang, then the Five

Phases or Elements 五行, the Eight Great Manifestations 八卦, the Ten Heavenly Stems 天干, the Twelve Earthly Branches 地支 (commonly known as the Chinese zodiac), and the sixty-four hexagrams of the I Ching. In mysterious synchronicity, there are also sixty-four codons in the nucleic acids of our genome. These sacred symbols contain all known and unknown phenomena of the cosmos, tracing light-years between constellations and millimeters between the human vertebrae.

In Chinese medicine, our bodies are microcosms of all existence. At all scales of human comprehension, matter and energy flow through phases of Yin and Yang, Wood, Fire, Metal, Earth, and Water. Qi 氣, Blood 血, Essence 精, and Bodily Fluids 津液 are constantly in motion through the intricate meridian system of the human form. The flow of air through our respiratory tracts is a mirror of the changing seasons. Ancient Chinese scholars knew that change is constant and that it is in skillful adaptation that we thrive.

This insight transcends borders, as witnessed in the work of twentieth-century Black science fiction author Octavia Butler. Her call to "shape change" and align with nature's transformations vibrates in harmony with the Daodejing. I invoke Butler's legacy to remind us that Daoist principles are not fixed in faded characters from thousands of years ago, nor are they separate from contemporary struggles for justice. In these pages, we will trace the threads that weave ancient knowledge with today's challenges.

WHAT IS THIS BOOK, ANYWAY?

This text is a recipe, a map, and a manual for people to return to dignity. Using the fivefold metaphysical framework of Daoism, this book outlines a process to heal, engage in embodiment, self-reflect, practice ancestor work, and take action to change your world for the better. The visualizations, remedies, meditations, and exercises are meant to empower you with tools for transformation. It is by no means an exhaustive, representative Chinese medical or Daoist text, but more like a care package from a dear friend. I chose from the treasure trove of my paternal heritage what I find most practical and accessible for folks who don't have the time or money to learn classical Chinese and meditate an hour every day.

These pages can supplement, but not replace, healing with a trained practitioner of Chinese medicine. The acupoints you locate on yourself are for pressure only, not needling. Your fingers or an ethically sourced crystal can initiate a potent healing response. Herbs, too, are powerful and deserving of respect. Unlike European herbalism, formulas are more common than single herb remedies in Chinese medicine. I see this as a beautiful counterpoint to individualism and a testament to collective power. The plant, animal, and mineral substances of the Chinese pharmacopeia can interact with each other and with prescription medications. Because of potential herb-drug interactions and contraindications based on patient constitution and symptoms, I strongly recommend consulting a trained Chinese herbalist as opposed to self-medicating with pills from the internet or a local health food store. This is one way to honor the generations of ancestors who researched and preserved this knowledge.

The remedies I share in the following pages are mostly "food herbs" you can keep in your pantry, which are less potent than purely medicinal substances. Kitchen herbalism also deserves respect, so please be cautious with any item your body is not acquainted with, and test small amounts to avoid allergic reactions. Use them in moderation.

What this book is:
- Sunlight refracted through the prism of my soul
- Introduction to my interpretation of the Five Elemental Phases五行
- Layperson tools for personal healing and cultivation
- An introduction to the wide world of texts, knowledge, and wisdom beyond this book

What this book isn't:
- A translation of specific texts
- A medical textbook
- An authoritative resource on all Daoist metaphysics
- A new innovative discovery
- A compendium of esoteric secrets

HOW TO USE THIS BOOK

Throughout this book, I offer prompts for reflection through creative alchemy. It's a good idea to begin this journey with a blank notebook or journal so that you have a space for written contemplation. I invite you to respond through writing, drawing, collage, movement, song, or other outlets of expression. The more courageously honest you are able to be, the deeper healing you will experience. The physical act of drawing or writing personalizes your reflection and allows for a more embodied, integrated experience. Rather than an intellectual treatise or a pamphlet to skim and forget, this book is meant to guide you inward to alchemize your healing potential.

The meditations interspersed throughout this text are designed to harness the healing power of visualization and complement the exercises. There are no set hand postures or sitting positions for these meditations, which are meant to be accessible for beginners and experienced meditators alike.

Simply allowing your imagination to follow the words is more than enough. The colors, archetypes, and energies correspond to ancient archetypes. You can read them silently as you sit in a comfortable place. You can also record yourself reading the meditation and then play it back for yourself.

If at any point you experience distress of any kind, stop immediately. Stomping your feet on the floor while placing your hands on your heart and counting ten breaths can be a simple way to ground yourself.

CORE PRINCIPLES

This book is designed to guide you through the generating cycle of the Five Elements on a journey of ancestral healing. Yet there are always many concurrent cycles unfurling simultaneously within our own bodies and the ecosystems that sustain us. Chinese medicine teaches that life force circulates through the twelve primary meridians of the body every twenty-four hours, while the Heavenly Stems and Earthly Branches take sixty years to complete. A single acupuncture needle can connect rivers of energy shaped by these timelines, turning a stream into a waterfall. For this reason, you may find yourself spiraling backward or forward within the sequence. Within your own being, you are the expert on what you need. The remedies and exercises contained within these pages are golden needles for you to heal yourself. As you make use of these tools, I invite you to consider the following core principles.

The Body Knows

As you go through this book, actively listen to somatic responses. How does your breathing change? Where do you feel tension? Openness? The body's messages are a compass toward our truth. Grounding deeply in one's own skin without slipping into navel-gazing can be a challenge. Yet it is worthwhile to feel into that delicate balance.

After each exercise and ritual, I invite you to set a five-minute timer to embody whatever feelings come up. Allow the emotions to move through and out with sound, breath, physical movement, and tears. We are built to release—we exhale, urinate, and defecate because our bodies must externalize waste matter. Emotional and spiritual waste can become, metaphorically, backed up when we hold in our feelings. Holding in waste is toxic, so allow yourself to let it all out.

Discomfort Is Different from Danger

Should physical-emotional distress arise, take a moment to feel the earth beneath you. Check in with your senses. If you are physically safe, consider that you could be experiencing discomfort rather than danger. Trauma can make it hard for the body to differentiate between the two, so please be gentle with yourself. Baby steps beyond comfort toward your growth zone are courageous, and they add up. Little by little, what was once intolerable can become manageable.

Systemic Harm Is Real, Yet We Can Make a Difference

Children's books and movies usually depict a singular villain with malicious intent, defeated quickly by a hero or small heroic team. From a young age, many of us internalize that there are "good guys" and "bad guys," and we are the former.

These attitudes don't reflect the research on systemic harm. Large-scale violence continues through societal institutions that ordinary people support without conscious intent to inflict pain. Individual conscious bigotry is not the prime driver of this profound injustice, and there is no single "bad guy" to defeat for a happy ending. Social structures perpetuate inequity, and to continue doing so, all they need is for most people to do nothing.

This is why it's not helpful to focus on personal intent or get stuck in feelings of shame. Those tendencies keep us out of constructive action and maintain the status quo. Grasping the breadth and depth of violence on a global scale can feel debilitating, particularly when we assume that a single individual should be able to fix it all. The good news is in the bad news: nobody can end all suffering single-handedly. If that were possible, surely our ancestors would have already done so. But while heroic figures throughout history may not have eradicated injustice in their lifetimes, their choices left a tremendous impact. Their legacies charge us, the living, with a responsibility to give our all.

In circular, regenerative processes, what is stagnant is renewed through ongoing release. When our tree kindred shed autumn leaves, mycelium compost them into rich topsoil for saplings. Small, consistent action in your own circle of influence can radiate through your relationships. If you feel immobilized by the state of the world, check to see if you have defaulted to the expectation that you or anyone else could be a superhero. Why not be a mushroom on the forest floor instead? Detoxify the soil around you, little by little, day by day.

The Work Is for Children We May Never Meet

The structures of injustice we confront today have centuries-old roots. Generation after generation strives to transform society for the better, and the work is always incomplete. In releasing the expectation that we can fix it all ourselves, we gain humility. We take our place in a long line of ancestors and create an inheritance for those to come. (For those of us who believe in reincarnation, we are also planting seeds for futures we hope to experience!)

Reconnection Is True Power

Audre Lorde wrote, "In order to perpetuate itself, every oppression must corrupt or distort those various sources of power within the culture of the oppressed that can provide energy for change." In my own life, the forces of white supremacy, patriarchy, homophobia, Orientalism, and transphobia systematically blocked me from accessing my Taiwanese cultural inheritance. The resources I share in the pages that follow are treasures that I fought for, decade after decade. With each herb, meridian, and meditation, I feel more at home in my cells.

You don't have to identify as an oppressed person to experience disconnection from the full vibrance of your life force. Many cultures have identified energy centers on the human body, from chakras to energy centers 丹田. In Daoism, these are "elixir fields" that can connect to celestial realms, other living beings, and the regenerative strength of the earth. In the crown of the head is the upper elixir field, which can gather heavenly energy from the stars and planets. The chest cavity is the cradle of the middle elixir field, where we connect on the horizontal axis to our loved ones and other earthly beings. The pelvic cavity holds the lower elixir field, a deep wellspring of ancestral vitality that roots down into the center of the earth.

Cultures worldwide have distinct but similar understandings of these energy sources. Societies on all continents honor sovereign relationships to land, interpersonal bonds, and a flow of prayer to the invisible planes of existence.

DEFINITIONS

The metaphysical language of this book is Daoist. The cosmological worldview these principles emerge from is ancient, distilled from millennia of observation of the natural environment. These concepts apply far beyond the Chinese mountains where many Daoist scholars lived, because acupuncture and herbal medicine consistently provide results in people of all backgrounds. It would take many lifetimes to learn all there is to know about

Daoism, and this book does not attempt to encompass its vastness. My goal is to draw from this bottomless well of wisdom and share what can support readers in catalyzing ancestral healing and alignment with their purpose. The definitions that follow are like a finger pointing at the moon, as the Shurangama Sutra teaches. Direct your gaze toward the moon itself.

道 **Dao:** The classic texts tell us that any attempt to describe the Dao will be incomplete. The first chapter of the Daodejing teaches that the unnamable reality of Dao, beyond any definition, is the source of all existence. We can always return to this source when we go within, stilling our bodies and minds. Often translated as "the way" or "the road," Dao can be a metaphorical or literal path. In spiritual cultivation, practitioners may seek to become one with Dao, an indescribable experience of enlightenment.

This great mystery is at the heart of Lee Dao-Ling 李道玲, the Chinese name I received from my grandma Suchin Lin Lee.

The umbrella of Daoism covers an array of schools of practice with great diversity of thought. A rich canon of texts is a living archive of millennia of lively theological and metaphysical discussion on the Dao. This book does not presume to summarize or represent the oceanic scope of Daoism, and I encourage interested readers to look beyond these pages to the work of knowledgeable authors and translators who specialize in the field. I am not interested in debates about purity or superiority that pit different teachers and philosophies against each other, so you will not find any of that here.

The overlap between Chinese folk religion and Daoism, Buddhism, and Confucianism is another source of debate. I will also not be participating in this controversy. What is important to me is that rural practices be honored for their vital role in community survival. I value the ancestral memory, competency, and wisdom of ordinary people's oral tradition just as much as a primordial text.

氣 **Qi:** Robert Hoffman explains Qi as "both the process and the product of life." Often reduced only to life force energy, Qi is much more. Everything has Qi, from an ant to the planet Jupiter and everything in between. For the purpose of this book, it might be helpful to draw parallels to the Yoruba concept of àṣe or the South Asian principle of prāna. All that you can perceive, and what you cannot, is connected in what Hua-Ching Ni calls "the universal energy net."

陰陽 **Yin and Yang:** These are relative terms that describe observable polarities. Yin is comparable to Òyèkú and Yang to Ogbè in Yoruba metaphysics, and both of these ancient systems predate the 0-1 binary code of computer technology. Unlike George Lucas's depiction of "the dark side" fighting and seeking to exterminate the Jedi in the Star Wars movies, Yin and Yang are utterly complementary and equal in value. Their creation and support of each other sustains all life. The 太極圖 Taijitu symbol, popularly called "yin-yang," is in constant motion. When you see the dark and light teardrops perfectly fit together, know that they are dancing in multiple dimensions, transforming and generating the beautiful diversity of existence.

Yin and Yang are not fixed qualities, but dynamic and deeply relational. The moon is Yin relative to the sun but Yang relative to the night sky around it. When Yang reaches its highest point, at high noon or the summer solstice, it gives way to Yin. Midnight is the beginning of the turn toward the light. Scholars of Chinese etymology translate Yin as "the shady side of a hill" and Yang as the sunbathed aspect. During a single day, the Yin and Yang sides of the hill will change as the sun proceeds along the ecliptic.

As a nonbinary person, I reject the oversimplified equivalence of Yin with women and Yang with men. Gender-nonconforming people in China use the term yinyangren to describe their experience of their own being, and Chinese medical theory ascribes both Yin and Yang aspects to the organs. All of us embody many levels of Yin and Yang, from Absolute Yin 厥陰風木 to Great Yang 太陽寒水. These Six Stages of Transformation in the human body are observable phenomena that emerge from the Six Cosmic Qi, cyclical forces of existence. Yin and Yang are inseparable from Five Element Theory and the sixty-four hexagrams of the I Ching. Although Yin and Yang are a polarity, I do not believe them to be equivalent to the gender binary.

As embodiments of ever-transforming Yin and Yang, we are always connected to the cosmic sources of nourishment (Yin) and vitality (Yang). The earth below is constantly supporting us, and the sun is always shining upon us, even when clouds appear to hide its light. To replenish and harmonize these fountains of strength, we can do a simple movement called Return of Qi or Connecting Heaven and Earth.

1. Sit or stand straight, so that your spine stretches toward the sky.

2. With your palms facing up, extend your hands out to the sides of your body and slowly raise them.

3. When your hands are about a foot above the top of your head, turn your palms to face the crown of your head and bring your hands toward each other until your fingertips are a few inches apart.

4. Slowly let your hands float down in front of your body along the centerline. When you reach your waist, you may begin again.

This list is an introduction to some of the polarities that can express Yin and Yang.

YIN	YANG
Night	Day
Sleep	Waking
Darkness	Brightness
Substance	Activity
Winter	Summer

五行 **Five Elements or Five Phases:** These energy configurations are a way of understanding the process of change. Rather than fixed substances with an unchanging essence, they are sometimes translated as phases. As the moon progresses from new to full and back again, so does the cycle of Wood, Fire, Earth, Metal, and Water. In this book, the capitalized names of the elements refer to these metaphysical energies, not our more everyday understanding of the words.

Around us and within us, processes of elemental healing unfold. In the chapters to come, you will follow the generating sequence from spring to winter. Plants become Wood, ashes become Earth, the Earth gives Metal, and on Metal's surface condenses Water. However, the Five Elements also balance one another, preventing excess. Water checks Fire, Fire melts Metal, and so forth. These relationships maintain harmony on multiple scales of magnitude. Although the generating cycle of the Five Elements traditionally begins with Wood, I have chosen to start this book with Fire because it is the element of love. Amid tremendous tragedy and injustice, radical love is what gives life meaning.

八卦 **Eight Trigrams:** When gathered in trios, there are eight possible energetic configurations of Yin and Yang. Like Yin, Yang, and the Five Elements, these manifestations of change are prisms through which a person can understand reality. One exercise I do is to look around myself at any given moment and identify the trigrams present. As organizing principles of existence, they are all around us. The Eight Trigrams, like fractals, unfurl in mathematical synchronicity from fern to fjord.

The 八卦 Bagua symbol, literally translated as Eight Trigrams, is an extremely important tool in most Feng Shui schools. These fundamental energy arrangements have many esoteric meanings and functions, including protection. You may encounter an octagon with the Taijitu symbol surrounded by the Eight Trigrams located above a threshold in the Pre-Heaven

先天八卦 or Post-Heaven 後天八卦 configuration. The Eight Trigrams are connected to the Five Elements and are essential to Chinese anatomy, astrology, geomancy, and many other systems of understanding. The associations below barely dapple the surface of their depths.

☷ 坤 **Kun:** Earth, Mother

☴ 巽 **Xun:** Wood or Wind, Eldest Daughter

☲ 離 **Li:** Fire, Middle Daughter

☱ 兌 **Dui:** Lake, Youngest Daughter

☶ 艮 **Gen:** Mountain, Youngest Son

☵ 坎 **Kan:** Rushing River, Middle Son

☳ 震 **Zhen:** Thunder, Eldest Son

☰ 乾 **Qian:** Heaven, Father

臟腑 **Chinese Medical Organs:** It's important to understand that the organs in Chinese medicine and Daoism are not equivalent to those in biomedicine. I capitalize Liver, Spleen, Kidney, and so on to make this distinction clear. Biomedicine saves countless lives and is a system in its own right, as is Chinese medicine. In these pages, we will engage with the esoteric, spiritual, and energetic properties of physiology that biomedicine does not address.

五神 **Five Spirits:** According to the teachings of Jeffrey C. Yuen, an unformed Spirit takes form to experience physical existence, and this process of slowing vibration creates the physical body. Even in the material sphere, spiritual energy is still present.

FU XI
Earlier Heaven

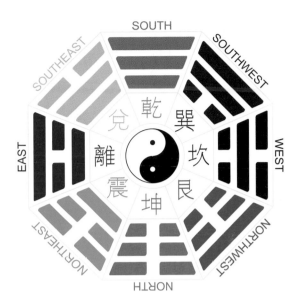

KING WEN
Later Heaven

Daoist texts locate divinity within the human form, with as many as thirty-six thousand gods inhabiting the body. This spiritual plurality has liberatory potential for nonbinary people who use they/we pronouns. Among this mystical throng, the deities of the five Yin organs are sometimes referred to as the Five Spirits 五神. In the chapters that follow, you will get to know these energies in relationship to the elemental phases they represent. They are the Ethereal Soul, Heart Spirit, Intellect, Corporeal Soul, and Willpower.

魂 **Ethereal Soul:** The Ethereal Soul is an aspect of consciousness that enters the body after birth and continues after physical death. Associated with the Liver and Wood, the Ethereal Soul dances and swirls with psychic animacy. This intuitive force thrives in constant motion, flowing through the dreamscape and our creative endeavors. Some say that human beings have three Ethereal Souls, while other animals and plants have fewer. The Ethereal Soul is a Yang energy, as is the Heart Spirit.

心神 **Heart Spirit/Shen:** The Heart Spirit gives us conscious, rational awareness and the capacity to make meaning of our experiences. This celestial center processes all our emotions and experiences during the day, and rests in our bloodstream at night. It is the center of spiritual and psychological development. Rooted in the Heart and embodying Fire, the Heart Shen unifies and integrates the other spirits. Confucian scholars ascribed this spirit with the qualities of a sovereign ruler, governing the divine court of the body.

意 **Intellect:** The Intellect governs intent and intellectual activity. Located in the Spleen and the Earth element, the Intellect directs and regulates thought. If you've ever experienced indigestion before a final exam, you know the relationship between study and stomach. Herbal formulas for students often include ingredients to support the Spleen and Intellect. Centrally located in the human trunk, the Intellect and Earth element digestive system are neutral, neither Yin nor Yang.

魄 **Corporeal Soul:** The Corporeal Soul is a Yin spirit inseparable from the body. In death, the Corporeal Soul returns to matter, while the Ethereal Soul lives on. Dwelling in the Lung and embodying Metal energy, the Corporeal Soul supports the Yang spirits by providing physical structure. Profoundly related to the Ethereal Soul, the Corporeal Soul gives form so that the Yang facets of consciousness can have a human experience. In some schools of thought, humans have seven Corporeal Souls.

志 **Willpower:** The Willpower resides in the Water element, stewarding ancestral wisdom and strength in the Kidney energetic system. A Yin spirit, the Willpower dwells with the inherited Essence 精 of many generations. It is the determination of the Willpower that drives us to overcome obstacles and fulfill our callings.

經絡 **Meridian System:** This channel network suffuses the human body, from the sensitive hairs of the epidermis to the marrow in our bones. While these rivers of energy flow alongside biomedical substances like blood and lymph, the meridians are not the central nervous system, the cardiovascular system, or any other biomedical structure. It's important to honor the integrity of Chinese medicine as a system that does not need external validation or explanation.

Meridians connect the entirety of the body in a web of animacy. From one dawn to the next, Qi courses through all twelve primary channels/meridians (these are interchangeable translations of the same concept). Replenishing where there is depletion and reducing where there is excess, the channels are meant to glide steadily, in rhythm with the cosmos. The Yellow Emperor's Inner Classic 黃帝內經 teaches that all forms of disease can be understood as stagnation. Embodied practices such as qigong and taijiquan prevent blockage and support continuous, rejuvenating motion.

All humans carry seas, lakes, and tributaries within us. Categorized by Yin, Yang, and the Five Phases, the primary channels deliver vitality to the organs. While this unceasing stream makes day-to-day life possible, the eight extraordinary meridians gather reservoirs for times of difficulty. When you gaze out an airplane window, notice the symmetry between the branching, converging waters and the veins in your own wrist.

腧穴 **Acupoints or acupuncture points:** If a channel is blocked, an acupuncturist may insert a pin at a critical juncture to restore the free flow of Qi. Returning to the view from an airplane window, imagine that one of the

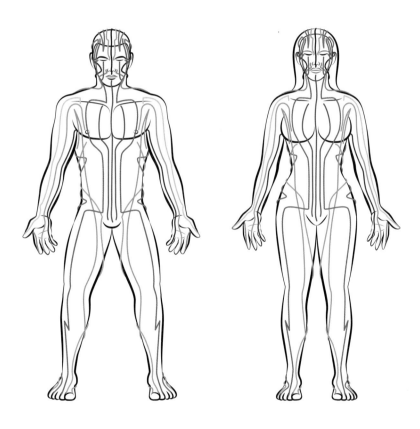

rivers is frozen. A pillar of sunlight descends from the sky to melt the ice and irrigate the watershed. On a smaller scale, that is what happens in an acupuncture session.

Another metaphor my teachers have shared is that of a key and a lock. Over thousands of years of trial and error, in the largest and most populous continent in the world, clinicians have identified specific sites on the body that are highly effective. Acupuncture points are keys that can unlock greater vitality and relieve pain. Called ah-shi ("Yes, there!") points, they are sometimes tender locations that consistently produce observable results. Mummified remains dating back five thousand years show tattoos near classical acupuncture points.

I personally love to envision the points as stars and the meridians as nebulae, the cosmos painted on my skin. In esoteric Daoist practice, meridian tracing invokes specific colors that correspond to celestial energies. Instead of comparing my external appearance to oppressive beauty standards, I close my eyes and see my skin illuminated by rainbows. Points shimmer along my limbs, patterns of starlight I share with all humanity.

臟腑 **Yin and Yang Organs:** Chinese medical theory holds that there are six Yin and six Yang entities in the body. Interconnected by the twelve primary meridians, these organs store and transport essential substances. Woven together with physiological functions are metaphysical actions that reflect cosmic patterns of change.

SPIRITUAL BYPASSING

This is a spiritual book, so we need to talk about spiritual bypassing. Psychotherapist John Welwood introduced this term decades ago as the use of "spiritual ideas and practices to sidestep personal, emotional 'unfinished business,' to shore up a shaky sense of self, or to belittle basic needs, feelings, and developmental tasks." When life feels overwhelming, astral travel becomes appealing. Trauma work, interpersonal conflict, structural oppression, and other facets of human existence can be incredibly painful. It is understandable to seek relief by running away toward apparent enlightenment—I certainly have done so myself. Ultimately, however, it's like charging expenses to a credit card. The payment comes due, with interest.

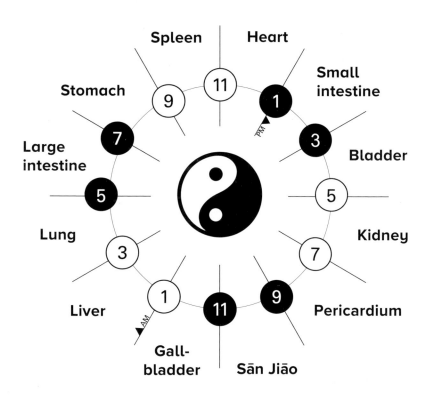

AUTHOR'S NOTE

If the motivation to seek solace in Daoism, Buddhism, or yoga is to escape the work of reconnection with European Earth-centered traditions, it can get messy. Projecting unmet needs onto spiritual systems that seem strange and attractive happens unconsciously, but the effects can be harmful. Many ancient cultures practiced in similar ways thousands of years ago. The most generative cross-cultural encounters are grounded in equity and mutual respect, not escapism or illusion.

Daoism teaches that the unnamable origin is the root of diverse phenomena, so we share a common origin. Every thing is trying to return to the Source. Acupoints and traditional herbs work on all bodies, regardless of phenotype. The integral realm welcomes and blesses those who come with sincere hearts and diligent cultivation. At the same time, we live in societies where centuries-old ideas of human worth are still heartbreakingly accurate predictors of length and quality of life.

The hexagrams of the I Ching demonstrate this concurrent reality. The fact they all spring forth from Yin and Yang does not render them identical. Their distinctions allow them to provide human beings with greater insight so that we can adapt to change. Similarly, my current incarnation is but one possible arrangement of water molecules and stardust. Although I share a common ancestor and most of my DNA with my fellow humans, I am also unique. Audre Lorde taught that denial of difference causes suffering, not difference itself. Problems arise when we refuse to "follow the rightness of the way each thing already is," as Brook Ziporyn translates Zhuangzi. Denial of difference is a way of ignoring the Dao of each thing.

Whether or not you are Chinese, I invite you to connect with the wisdom of Traditional Chinese Medicine that I share, and to respect my boundaries. Because you have compensated me—a Taiwanese diaspora person reclaiming my ancestral medicine—I see this as a just exchange. The funds you invested in this book help reduce the debt I'm taking on for acupuncture school and allow me to offer healing and facilitation work on a sliding scale in service of economic justice. It would be inappropriate to use this text as the foundation of a paid energy healing practice or represent oneself as an expert in Daoist metaphysics. Learning these traditions takes time and study with lineage bearers.

I am the eldest descendant of Dr. William Tsung-Liang Lee, his father Dr. Ting-Chien Lee, and other doctors before them. From Fujian province to the windswept island of Kinmen, from rural Miaoli County to bustling Taipei, my paternal ancestors have practiced medicine. The methods and knowledge of Chinese medicine are inseparable from the enormous, complex, imperfect, magnificent whole of Asian cultures.

This book contains the wisdom of generations in my blood. I offer these resources because, on a spiritual level, all of us are kindred in light. Because we encounter each other in physical form, we work within contexts of power. As the medicine of my ancestors blesses your life, I expect reciprocity. Not simply in the money you paid for this book, but in the way you show up for Asian diaspora communities.

We are human and whole. The healing power of our folkways is inseparable from the memories we carry in our bones.

Part One

FIRE

火

土

金

水

木

Sacred Initiation

Illuminates the hidden

Immolates what is no longer needed

Sends sacred smoke to the listening Heavens

Planet: Mars 火星 Huǒ Xīng

Direction: South

Season: Summer

Guardian: Vermilion Bird 南方朱雀 Nán Fāng Zhū Què

Lunar mansions: Well 井 Jǐng, Ghost 鬼 Guǐ, Willow 柳 Liǔ, Star 星 Xīng, Extended Net 張 Zhāng, Wings 翼 Yì, Chariot 軫 Zhěn

Color: Red

Emotion: Joy

Organs: Heart, Small Intestine, Pericardium, Triple Warmer 三焦 Sān Jiāo

Spirit: Heart Spirit 神 Shen

Trigram: ☲ Fire 離 Li

Affirmation: I am regal and radiant.

CHAPTER 1

SELF-SOOTHING

As we begin investigating the elements, here are some things to consider. First, you can begin anywhere. You embody all of the elements, and all of these energies are constantly flowing in relationship to one another. The sequence I follow here is just one way to experience the elemental cycle. Second, what draws you, and what kindles resistance? Some exercises or meditations might immediately appeal to you, while others might spark refusal. I suggest following desire and excitement, and journaling on what exercises might bring up unwillingness. What lies beneath the resistance? Surfacing the emotions below may be enlightening.

Fire's connection to the Heart makes it especially important for emotional and physical regulation, which I refer to in this book as self-soothing. Chinese medical texts, particularly those influenced by Confucianism, describe the Heart 心 as the emperor of the microcosmic human body. Although the other four Yin organs embody aspects of human emotional-spiritual existence, it is the Heart Spirit 心神 that consciously experiences and makes meaning. Emotional distress can fall under many diagnoses in Chinese medicine, including "phlegm fire misting the Heart," "Heart blood deficiency," and so on. Treatment protocols include herbs and points that calm the Heart Spirit as well as the Pericardium, a Fire organ that protects the Heart both physically and emotionally.

Self-soothing helps our bodies manage distress when we are out of our window of tolerance. This model of understanding emotion regulation comes from psychiatrist Dan Siegel, who developed the window metaphor to describe how different people have varied capacities for dealing with discomfort. Everyone has their own baseline and a range of situations outside that emotional baseline that lead to hypoarousal or hyperarousal. Hypoarousal describes reactions like feeling numb, while hyperarousal includes outwardly directed strategies like fight-or-flight. In these states, the limbic system overrides the conscious mind in an attempt to protect the body from danger. People who have lived through trauma, chronic stress, neglect, or abuse may enter a dysregulated state—an off-balance sensation that precedes hypo- or hyperarousal—based on circumstances that don't seem that serious to others. It is possible to expand your window of tolerance, but it's important to choose compassion for the size of your current window.

Fire element practices to return to your window of tolerance are available even if you can't afford a Five Element acupuncture treatment. To increase your awareness of your inner Fire, pay attention to the center of your chest. If you have a battery-powered candle (or a supervised real candle), it can be helpful to spend some time watching the flickering light. Facing the south, feel for Mars, which is not a planet of war in Chinese cosmology but an energy that can provide warmth and love. Visualize a gentle, comforting pink light traveling across the solar system and connecting with your heart. Reishi mushroom 靈芝 nourishes the Heart and helps with insomnia. Schisandra fruit 五味子 soothes agitated Heart Qi and benefits all Five Elements. Fire in excess is heat, which you can address by eating watermelon 西瓜. Remember that the phoenix, archetype of the element Fire and guardian of the south, is reborn from ashes. Despite experiences that have burned you, the element

Fire can remind you of joy, love, and resurrection. The Heart is also in the center of the middle elixir field, where we connect outward to other living beings with love. In this book, I invite you to lead from your heart.

Laughter is Fire medicine best taken with people you love. The sound of the Fire element, laughter is the vibrational manifestation of joy, the Fire element's cardinal emotion. In Daoist tradition, the healing sound for the Heart is *Haa*. Although traditionally exhaled in a meditative practice, notice how you naturally make the *ha* sound when you burst into laughter. The scientific community has identified biomedical benefits of humor on emotional and physiological health. When you allow yourself to find delight in silliness and lightness, your inner Fire frolics brightly. If you notice yourself spending more time than you'd like on social media or watching "shallow" television, perhaps you're unconsciously responding to a deficiency of Fire energy within. Let yourself experience levity to keep the flame from dying out. Once you feel that you've had enough, consider other ways to feed the Fire. Playing games with kids is an excellent way to reconnect with exuberance. Just for a little while, put aside the heaviness of adult concerns and allow Fire to dance freely.

When we embrace another person, our hearts connect on the horizontal axis. A hug also brings the Conception Vessel of one person in contact with the other, applying gentle acupressure along the meridian. The Conception Vessel is an extraordinary channel also called the Sea of Yin, located on the Yin frontal aspect of the body. For these reasons, a hug from someone you trust can provide Yin feelings of nourishment, nurturing, care, and support. It's important for infants to have skin-to-skin contact with safe caregivers, Conception Vessel to Conception Vessel. This physical experience of bonding helps with primary attachment formation, which impacts health outcomes for a lifetime. Effie Chow, a world-renowned energy healer and humanitarian, recommended several belly laughs and hugs per day for optimal health.

Our arms and hands flow with the alchemical energy that differentiates us from other species. Freed from weight-bearing because our species is bipedal, the arms can lift and carry items that we grasp with opposable thumbs. These evolutions allow humans to create shelter and shape the environment around us. From a Chinese medical perspective, the arms and hands flow with the Fire and Metal meridians of the Lung, Large Intestine, Pericardium, Triple Warmer 三焦, Small Intestine, and Heart. At the fingertips lie the extraordinary Ten Diffusions 十宣 points, clinically indicated for loss of consciousness. Our fingertips are also places where Yin and Yang meridians meet and change polarity. In the blacksmith's forge, Fire and Metal work together to kindle flames, transform matter, and make tools. These limbs are powerful, allowing us to do things that other creatures cannot. Daoist practice involves specific hand positions in healing and cultivation, as do many traditional modalities around the world.

This power is in your hands. Rub them together to generate Qi, then hold them over your eyes while inhaling down into your Heart. You can also place your warmed palms on parts of your body that desire touch and direct your intent toward healing. Bending your index and middle finger at the joint closest to your hand, grasp the thumb and fingers of the opposite hand at the root. Pulling gently but firmly away from the hand, imagine that you are uncapping each one. You can imagine smoke wafting out, sludge dripping, or whatever metaphor works best for you.

The energetic potency of the hands gives acupressure its effectiveness. The points I share throughout this book respond to the Fire-Metal Qi in the fingers, and the Fire element points in this chapter are on the hand and arm. For acupressure, you may also use ethically sourced crystals, which have a long history in Chinese medical tradition. I recommend consulting L. J. Franks's *Stone Medicine: A Chinese Medical Guide to Healing with Gems and Minerals*.

Just as everyone's window of tolerance is different, everyone will need different methods to self-regulate (return to your window) and broaden their capacity to function in challenging moments. This chapter, and this book, are meant to support you in identifying what works for you. As people in recovery rooms say, "Take what you like and leave the rest." You will have your personal set of self-soothing practices, but here are a few suggestions to get started:

- Play your favorite songs or sounds.

- Repeat "I am safe," "I love me no matter what," and other reassuring words.

- Drop peppermint 薄荷 oil in your palms, rub your hands together, close your eyes, and inhale from your cupped hands.

- Open a citrus fruit to allow the scent to fill the room.

- Gently hold the crown of your head, the seat of your consciousness.

- Hug yourself softly.

- Stroke your own face, arms, or anywhere that feels comforting.

- Drink a cup of tea.

FIRE ACUPRESSURE

INNER PASS 內關

The Inner Pass 內關 opens up the chest, calms emotional upset, and benefits digestion. Placing the tip of your index finger on the wrist crease of the opposite hand, look at the proximal interphalangeal joint (the bigger one that is closer to the hand, not the fingertip) of the index finger. This is the location of the acupoint, right in the middle of the inner forearm. The Inner Pass 內關 treats chest and Heart issues, but it's imperative that you immediately seek Western medical attention if you experience chest pain that radiates along the left arm. Do not perform acupressure or seek acupuncture in these situations, because this is a warning sign of cardiac arrest.

THE SPIRIT GATE 神門

The Spirit Gate 神門 also benefits the Heart, and the same caution applies. Praised as the principal point to soothe the Heart Spirit, Spirit Gate 神門 is at the wrist joint below the pinky finger. Along the edge between the front and back of the hand, slightly closer to the palm, feel for a bony bump. Letting your finger fall off the bump slightly, toward the wrist crease, feel for a depression. Symptoms of mania, disorientation, insomnia, and agitation would all indicate the use of these two points.

Sanctuary Visualization

Let's begin by drawing attention to your connection to the earth. Whether you are sitting or lying down, begin to release tension downward. Close your eyes. Allow heaviness to sink out of you with gravity's support. Gravity is an embrace that is just right—not tight enough to crush us, not loose enough to let us fly away. Let the earth receive what is too much for you to hold.

Feel a waterfall of moonlight from above. Opalescent moonbeams pour down upon you, cleansing your energy body from the crown of your head to your feet. After coursing through your human vessel, the moonlight seeps into Mother Earth.

You see a circle of your favorite trees form around you. Are they cedar? Sequoia? Redwood? Olive? Birch? Eucalyptus? Banyan? Baobab?

Vines begin to weave the trees together. Are they morning glories? Yellow squash? Grapevines? Honeysuckle?

Feel a soft cushion of moss below. Can you hear the flow of a waterfall? Watch light flicker off the scales of koi fish in the pond. At the center of the clearing, you notice a mandala formed from crystals and flowers. Take a moment to kindle the flame in your firepit as the golden hour of sunset approaches.

Outside your clearing, protective beings stroll with power and purpose. Are they tigers? Elephants? Dragons?

Cradle your inner infant, and hold hands with your inner toddler. See, feel, and hear all past versions of yourself held in safety.

Say your name three times. This is the key that only you hold: your sacred name in your unique voice. This is your inner sanctuary. It belongs only to you and is yours whenever you need it.

When you're ready, stand on the crystal mandala. Take three deep breaths all the way to your pelvic floor. Begin to feel your toes, fingers, and body on the earth. Slowly return to your body and the space. Hand on heart, open your eyes whenever you are ready.

SELF-SOOTHING EXERCISE

For these prompts, as well as those throughout the rest of this book, I recommend designating a blank notebook to write your responses. Block out uninterrupted time to answer these questions mindfully and at your own pace.

1. How did I try to comfort myself when I was a child? How did the adults around me respond? What did I observe and internalize from those examples?

2. How do I manage difficult emotions and experiences now? When did I begin to use those coping mechanisms? Did previous generations of my family cope in similar ways? When did the patterns begin?

3. What messages did I internalize about the ways I self-soothe? As you write them out, evaluate: Is this true? Who told me this?

4. Is it now safe to return to self-soothing practices from childhood (for example, crying loudly when I feel sad instead of swallowing the tears)?

INNER PHYSICIAN

Harm reduction is a way of understanding coping mechanisms that have elements of self-sabotage but meet a deep need. Self-medicating is a way that the inner physician tries to heal. You might want to use different medicine now that you have other options, and you can administer that medicine with the Fire element's compassion.

Maladaptive coping mechanisms are often the best attempt we have at the time. We, and the caregivers we learned our habits from, were trying to meet our needs. Note whenever self-judgment arises, whether through intrusive thoughts or somatic responses such as hunched shoulders or the urge to bite your nails. Whatever habits and beliefs you have acquired in this lifetime served you at some point. They got you here, to this moment, with breath in your lungs, and for that alone they—and you—deserve respect.

On a piece of paper or in your journal, draw four columns. In the first column, list coping mechanisms that you have relied on over the years. I invite you to include socially sanctioned behaviors that can be detrimental to our well-being. For example: working long hours, smiling even if you don't feel happy, prioritizing achievement or productivity above your health, and so on. Label the next three columns as "How it has helped me," "How it harms me," and "How I feel about it."

I find it helpful to fill out one column at a time, from left to right, but you may prefer to go row by row. After you have completed all four columns, take a break. When you are ready, return to the page and consider whether you'd like to make any changes. If you decide you'd like to reduce your use of a self-soothing behavior, I suggest writing a thank-you note to that behavior first. Please be gentle with yourself and consider seeking support in the process.

Grounding Visualization

Find your meditation posture, your spine unfurling to the sky as the earth cradles you. Exhale with intent as you release tension. Bring your awareness to the crown of your head as the moon begins to anoint you with iridescent light. Can you feel the rainbow refracted beams pour through you? Allow the illumination to soothe your cells from crown to root. Close your eyes.

Take three deep breaths, filling your lungs with clean, restorative energy. Each time you exhale, release something you no longer need. Say your sacred chosen name three times and notice your sanctuary around you.

One of your younger selves smiles at you and takes you by the hand. They guide you toward a comfortable, soft seat or bed. What color is it? Are you sitting on a velvet cushion? A sparkly cloud? Another child version of you dashes over with a handpicked bouquet of flowers. What do you smell? Roses? Magnolia? Mmm, what else do you smell? It's your favorite food! A nurturing figure brings you a bowl of your preferred dish, beautifully presented in vibrant colors.

Drop into the delicious sensations as you feel satisfaction fill you up. The aromas and flavors permeate your being with contentment. Your eyes take in the blooming flowers, shimmering waterfall, and glorious sky above you. You hear children's carefree laughter, the rush and swirl of waters, and bright birdsong.

Revel in these sensory experiences for as long as you need. Allow your senses to fill your body with pleasure. How good can you possibly feel? There is more than enough for you and all your younger selves, with more to share.

When you feel abundantly satisfied, bask in that feeling. Let the deep sensation of satisfaction, contentment, and nourishment well up in your aura, surrounding and suspending you in that energy.

When you're ready, return to the central mandala of your sanctuary and say your name three times. Slowly return to your meditation practice space, wiggle your fingers and toes, and open your eyes.

CHAPTER 2

LOVE AS VITAL QI

My undergraduate work in Africana studies introduced me to Black feminism, which is grounded in a love ethic that I find to be the most sustainable energy source in the multiverse. A beautiful introduction to June Jordan's assertion that "love is lifeforce" can be found in Alexis Pauline Gumbs's body of work. Within my own body, I experience the Qi that gives me breath as solar radiance.

The sun's light animates all our plant and animal kin, whose bodies sustain our own. We exhale carbon dioxide and exchange it for oxygen from tree siblings. We are bound in a sacred relationship, sunlight transforming and moving through us all. You may not have had much experience of unconditional love. However, the breath in your lungs and food in your belly are evidence that planet Earth is providing for you. Receive this unconditional love with gratitude, and allow it to move out and beyond you.

WHAT IS LOVE?

When I talk about love as vital Qi, I am not referring to romance depicted by Hollywood production houses and Top 40 song lyrics. Love is not exclusive to romance. Radical love is action and transformation. As June Jordan emphasized, it is a vital principle of freedom.

Mitochondrial DNA passed down through maternal lines traces human ancestry back to a woman who lived in East Africa almost two hundred thousand years ago. Though many others of our species have walked this planet, only her descendants survived to the present day. For tens of thousands of years, her life force has carried *Homo sapiens* through all the horrors of recorded history and still others never written. Across countless generations, acts of radical love have kept our species alive. In the following exercise, you will clarify your personal definition of love to carry you through the inevitable challenges of life.

UNCONDITIONAL LOVE EXERCISE

1. What does unconditional love mean to me?

2. Have I experienced unconditional love?

3. What experiences felt most like unconditional love thus far in my life?

4. Through what places, people, works of art, animals, plants, music, and so on have I experienced unconditional love?

5. How do I feel in my body when I remember those experiences and sources of love?

6. How can I grieve my experiences of conditional love? When, with whom, and in what ways can I release my justified emotions (which may include sorrow, rage, and others)?

7. How do I express unconditional love to others?

Integration Visualization

As you begin your meditation, notice the points of contact where your body touches the earth. Release tension with each exhale, allowing gravity to take away all burdens that you cannot bear. Allow moonlight to gently wash through your body inside and out, an illuminating energy that soothes your cells and spirit.

As your lungs expand, allow your heart center to fill up with freedom. With each exhale, imagine that you are releasing constraints. When you say your name three times, you become aware of the sanctuary you have created.

You're in the center of your grove on the crystal mandala. Can you smell the flowers? Hear the waterfall? See the smiles on your younger selves' faces? Feel a gentle breeze tickle your skin?

A winged protector approaches you. Is this Pegasus? A phoenix? A condor? A dragon? The guide invites you to climb on its back. Together, you soar above your grove and begin to see your body from above. Your guide continues to fly higher, allowing you to see the hills and plant life where you live, bodies of water, cloud formations, and eventually all of planet Earth. You continue to zoom out, witnessing the solar system's radiant dance, shimmering spiral galaxies, vibrant nebulae, and the incredible abundance of stars. As you take in the breathtaking beauty around you, you hear exquisite, swelling music. The cosmos is vibrating in glorious harmony, and you feel utterly connected to all of it. You feel on a soul level that the ground of all being, the foundation of Existence, is liberatory unconditional love.

Your guide dives and dances through the cosmos and returns to Earth. As you notice your human body, you observe undeniable similarities between the cosmos and your being. You and your guide become smaller and smaller, perceiving the intricate, miraculous complexity of your organs, tissues, and cells. Golgi bodies remind you of nebulae, the nuclei like stars. You fly deeper, between protons, electrons, and neutrons that sing the same song as the whole of Existence. Within the subatomic particles of your being, you hear the symphony and see the star field of the whole. Feel deeply that you are inseparable from unconditional love.

When you're ready, your guide returns to the sanctuary, where you dismount. Your younger selves approach, bright-eyed, and ask to hear about your journey. How do you explain to them that they are made of unconditional love?

After hugging your younger selves, return to the center of your grove and say your name three times. Slowly return to your body, wiggling your toes and fingers.

In your journal, write your personalized unconditional love invocation. To align with the energy of Fire, you might recite this aloud on Sundays and Tuesdays, which correspond to the sun and Mars. Here are some suggestions:

- Call on benevolent forces such as the stars, moon, or Earth.

- Give thanks for all you have already received.

- Declare "I am" rather than "I want."

- Describe the love-filled life you long for in vivid sensory detail.

- Connect your thriving to the healing and liberation of all.

- Close with an affirmation that it is already so.

Vital Qi Ritual

1. *Light a candle if it is safe to do so.*

2. *As you draw in breath, remember that you are living sunlight. The warmth of your being itself is star song.*

3. *Bounce gently on the balls of your feet and, as when doing the hokey pokey, shake everything out.*

4. *Straighten and bend your fingers. Rotate your ankles, knees, hips, wrists, elbows, and shoulders. Gently glide your chin side to side along your collarbone.*

5. *Rub your hands together to create heat/Qi, then gently brush off your entire body.*

6. *Open your chest forward and pull your shoulders back, then open the scapulae for your wings to unfurl.*

7. *Read your invocation aloud one to three times.*

CHAPTER 3

INNER CHILD REUNION

Childhood trauma is a tragically common experience. Because our bodies remember violations at tender ages, these wounds sometimes burn when we are doing ancestor work. We began with self-soothing to equip you with tools to regulate neurobiological responses you might experience, and you can take a break at any time. Ancestral healing is not a race.

This chapter focuses on the inner child or inner children as essential partners in your healing. Internal family systems theory is a framework developed by psychologist Dick Schwartz, who noticed that his patients often talked about their "parts." This multiplicity is normal and can include younger selves. This book includes visualizations meant to appeal to young parts' vivid imagination. Younger selves are often profoundly honest and creative. When we listen to their observations and ideas, our lives can brighten and expand in possibility.

ATTACHMENT

As the human body and brain are developing, relationships are essential. Children's primary early attachments impact interpersonal connection for decades into adulthood. Relational experiences in the first several years of life have epigenetic impacts that alter brain function and structure. As *Homo sapiens*, we are social animals who need each other to survive.

As you journal on these prompts, reflect on your relationships to observe patterns. If you notice tendencies that you do not prefer, consider that they might have to do with attachment experiences in your early life. Without necessarily blaming your caregivers, can you find compassion for yourself as you navigate the natural human need for connection?

CONNECTION EXERCISE

1. Over the course of my life, whose attention have I longed for? What qualities do these people have in common?

2. What messages did I internalize about my natural need for connection?

3. What comes up when I consider asking for connection from my loved ones? Do I feel comfortable doing so? If not, what do I think might happen?

4. Whose attention do I desire? How do I feel about longing for connection from these people?

5. Do I know how to ask for connection from these people? If not, how can I learn and practice asking for what I need?

6. Who desires connection with me? How do I respond to those requests? Do I recognize their bids for connection?

Nurturing Visualization

As you enter the meditation space, settle into your body's contact with the earth. Let the crown of your head reach toward the heavens as gravity cradles your weight. Consciously allow the earth to hold you as your muscles slowly relax. The waterfall of moonlight anoints your head, washing over and through you in glowing, opalescent waves. Feel this gentle illumination nourishing every cell of your body as it pours through your core, pelvic cavity, legs, and feet.

Rooted and cleansed in moonlight, take three deep breaths. Allow your inhale to fill your belly, then fully exhale through the mouth as you release with a sound to express how you're feeling. Say your name three times, and notice you are in your sacred grove.

You feel a hand on your shoulder and turn to see a nurturing elder by your side who exudes a feeling of safety. You may recognize them as a supportive figure, or they may be an archetypal energy. You notice your inner children and younger selves around you. What are they doing? Are they playing? Are any of them trying to get your attention?

The elder guides you to a comfortable seat by the fire, and your younger selves gather around. The elder's lined face crinkles in a smile and their eyes overflow with warmth as they regard the little ones. Take the time to listen to any younger versions of you who want to be heard. Try to simply accept them for who they are, as they are. Show them your attention with a steady gaze of unconditional love. Do any of them crawl into your lap to cuddle? Can you rock them gently? If you're not sure how to comfort the little ones, look to the elder. Your elder models how to validate the younger parts of you with profound care. Stay here as long as you can, ideally until your younger selves curl up in contented sleep.

Can you feel that you are both the comforter and the comforted? Are you able to tap into the emotional experience of your younger selves, who have always deserved to be heard? Your elder takes your face in their hands and kisses your brow.

When you're ready, say your name three times and slowly return to the space.

Inner Child Ritual

1.   Choose a picture of yourself in childhood. If you don't like any photos you have, represent yourself through your preferred artistic medium.

2.   Find a place that can be your inner child's playroom. It might be a shelf, a box, or a tabletop. Place the picture there.

3.   Begin to surround the image with items that give you physical sensations of comfort, safety, and silliness. You might add toys, sweets, or children's books.

4.   Set aside time to spend with your inner child. You might enjoy a coloring book or play children's music and dance around. Put it on the calendar and keep your word to your inner child: don't flake. Try making time for regular playdates with your inner child while working on creative projects.

5.   Practice nondominant handwriting and drawing. Let your mind quiet, and notice what appears.

6.   Look into the eyes of your inner child, hug the picture, tell them you love them, or express care through another way that they prefer.

7.   Repeat regularly.

Part Two

EARTH

火

土

金

水

木

The Foundation

Supports all Life as we know it

Receives and transforms the old

Gives birth to the new

The ground of our being

Planet: Earth 地球 Dì Qiú and Saturn 土星 Tǔ Xīng

Direction: Center

Season: Late summer and seasonal transitions

Guardian: Yellow Dragon 黃龍 Huánglóng

Lunar mansions: None, the Earth is at the center of the twenty-eight Daoist constellations

Color: Yellow

Emotion: Thoughtfulness

Organs: Spleen, Stomach

Spirit: Intellect 意 Yi

Trigrams: ☷ Earth 坤 Kun, ☶ Mountain 艮 Gen

Affirmation: I am empowered and prepared.

CHAPTER 4

CONNECTING TO THE EARTH

As you connect with the Earth element, feel for your center. Notice if you find yourself leaning forward, hunching down, or tilting back and off your root. The element Earth is associated with the digestive organs as well as the way we process information. During this section, it's a good idea to eat mindfully, pay attention to your thoughts, and pause if you notice the mind racing. If you can, let your bare feet touch the soil. When worry or overthinking shows up, exhaling on the sound *Hu* can soothe the Intellect 意.

Nurturing life 養生 is an ancient Daoist practice that sustains a foundation of physical, emotional, and spiritual health. You can nurture life by practicing gratitude, eating local foods in season, resting more during the winter, and moving your body with gentle intent. You might reach out to relatives and compile recipes to make a family cookbook, keep a gratitude journal, or dance full out to your favorite songs. Caring for what gives your existence meaning forms a supportive spiritual foundation for other esoteric practices.

KITCHEN HERBALISM FOR THE EARTH ELEMENT

Fresh ginger 生姜 balances Yin and Yang in the center of the body and can stop vomiting. Jujube berry 大枣 can calm emotional distress while tonifying the Spleen and Stomach. Baked licorice root 甘草 especially benefits the Spleen and alleviates pain. Rice 粳米 tonifies Spleen Qi, and honey 蜂蜜 nourishes and protects the Earth organs. Jasmine 茉莉花 tea harmonizes the Earth organs and calms the nerves. Oregano 土茵陳 regulates Qi for sensations of distension, an Earth element symptom. Dried, aged tangerine peel 陈皮 can address nausea, epigastric or abdominal distension, and belching. Decoct these peels by boiling them in water over a flame. Do not use dried tangerine peel if you have a dry cough or a red tongue (not pink), and do not use it long-term. Garlic 大蒜 addresses mild food stagnation in the Spleen and Stomach, and it can help with edema when ground into a paste and applied on the navel. Joel Penner, expert on Chinese medicine and advisor to *Grey's Anatomy*, advised grinding garlic with salt and sesame oil to make a topical treatment for itching and rashes (never on the head, however).

The Earth element nourishes the body and also needs to be nourished. In Chinese medical theory, the Spleen prefers warmth, so you might have a cup of tea after your meals. Another simple way to support your Spleen and Stomach is to rub your hands together to generate heat, then gently circle your abdomen with your palm. Think of Winnie-the-Pooh, who is yellow (the Earth color), loves honey (the sweet Earth flavor), and rubs his belly. Trace upward on your right abdomen, across the body, and down on the left after meals to support digestion. If you are dealing with loose stool, reverse direction.

EARTH ACUPRESSURE

LEG THREE MILES 足三里

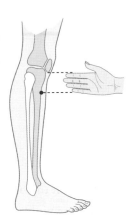

Leg Three Miles 足三里 harmonizes the Stomach, fortifies the Spleen, calms the spirit, and benefits original Qi. To locate Leg Three Miles 足三里, use two fingers to measure the length of your kneecap. Keep that measurement and move your top finger to the base of the kneecap. Where your lower finger touches the shin, let it fall off the bone in a lateral direction (away from the center of the body). Free your top finger and begin to palpate in this area. Where you feel tenderness or a physical response, you can apply pressure.

My professor tells a story of acupuncturists in China who put dozens of needles in the area because it is so beneficial, and many Chinese elders burn mugwort 艾叶 close to this point to support longevity. (This use of mugwort is not appropriate if a patient has heat symptoms like a rash, fever, or a red face.) Jin dynasty doctor Ma Dan-Yang included Leg Three Miles 足三里 in his list of eleven Heavenly Star Points that are most useful in clinical practice. As one of the most-researched acupuncture points, Leg Three Miles 足三里 is well documented in its efficacy in patient care.

THREE YIN INTERSECTION 三陰交

This point has wide clinical applications in treating emotional, digestive, urinary, and reproductive conditions. Locate this point by placing the edge of the pinky finger at the top of the medial malleolus, the bony protrusion on the inside of the ankle. Keep your four fingers together, palm touching the skin. At the level of the first joint of the middle finger (closest to the hand), find the distance between the outer edge of your index finger and the outer edge of your pinky. Feel for a depression near the bone of the tibia. This point is the meeting place of the Spleen, Liver, and Kidney channels, and it tonifies the Earth organs and treats issues throughout the body.

You and I are stardust, soil, and sunlight. In the web of life, we are bound to countless other beings whose death gives us life. The plants and animals we consume become part of us, their life force weaving into ours. When we live with integrity and serve justice, we honor the sacrifices of the beings who feed us. Nourishment begins in our bodies, but it is more than food. Nourishment is all that gives us life: a favorite song, a gentle embrace, a soft blanket, or the scent of homemade dinner.

NOURISHMENT EXERCISE

1. What places, foods, sounds, smells, sensations, textures, people, sights, and activities nourish me?

2. How do I feel in my body when I have all I need? If I haven't had this experience, what do I imagine it would feel like?

3. Have I experienced nourishment in this lifetime? How do I feel about its abundance or lack?

4. What activities and habits do I feel ready to replace with choices that nourish me? Which do I not feel ready to replace? Can I ask myself, without judgment, why?

5. What structural changes need to happen for me and my communities to experience nourishment?

6. What boundaries do I need to set to protect my nourishment?

CREATING SANCTUARY

Earth is home. Our species has no other. Billionaires who seek another planet after laying waste to this one are profoundly misguided. If we can't survive here without destroying ourselves, there is nowhere else we can go. This miracle of a planet in the "Goldilocks zone" between roasting and freezing, where liquid water birthed life, is already a sanctuary in deep space. You and I and all animate life are children of this planet, and we belong here. We are never entitled to take over others' ancestral lands, but as *Homo sapiens*, we have a right to exist on Earth. We deserve to feel at home on this globe.

All of us come from ancestors who had a sacred relationship with Earth at one point. Our bodies are the transformed matter of this planet, and thus we are its children. Grounding our bodies in this truth allows us to show up for meaningful action long-term.

Your body is sovereign ground formed from Earth's matter. You are also sunbeam in motion, the transformed rays of the sun's light. The very mitochondria in your cells are miracles. To create sanctuary, the following exercise is meant to help you ground in the stardust of your skin.

GROUNDING EXERCISE

1. What does safety feel like? Sound like? Smell like? Taste like? Look like?

2. Was home safe? Why?

3. What does home mean to you?

4. Are you displaced from ancestral homelands? If so, where was home for your ancestors?

5. What steps can you take to create safety and home for your inner children?

6. What are the boundaries of your space? If you cohabit with others, is there a closet you can call your own? A shelf?

7. What symbols of protection did your ancestors use? Whatever the size of your space, I invite you to use symbols and intent to consecrate and differentiate inside from outside. Your sacred space can be your own body.

8. How did your ancestors spiritually cleanse space? Take some time to research. How often is it feasible for you to spiritually cleanse your sanctuary? If it would feel supportive, perhaps put a reminder in your calendar to do so each moon cycle. If your sanctuary is your body, consider bathing with intention.

9. What images and objects bring your soul delight and solace? If you haven't already, begin to gather symbols and shapes that kindle joy and comfort in a physical space that is your own.

10. What sounds and words touch your heart? When can you make time to listen? Consider doing so when you are in your sanctuary.

11. Where in your body do you feel most at home? If there isn't a part of your body that feels safe, that's okay. Where in your body would you like to feel more at home?

12. What grounding objects (pebbles, crystals, pendants, rings) can you carry on your body to cultivate a greater sense of home? Note: please source crystals ethically and avoid appropriating sacred symbols from traditions that are not your own.

13. What phrases can you say to yourself when you need to ground yourself? What words call you home to yourself?

14. Are there people whose presence feels like home to you? How can you feel their care even when they are not physically with you? A photo, friendship bracelet, or other physical object can help with this connection.

Centering Visualization

Take a few deep breaths to release tension into the ground below. Begin to relax the muscles in your face, neck, and shoulders. Bring attention to the upper arms, then the forearms, and all the way to your fingertips. Soften your upper back and chest, then your abdomen and middle back. On a long exhale, relax your lower back and lower abdomen. Allow your thighs to loosen, then your calves, and finally your feet.

Envision the soles of your feet glowing brass-gold and the radiance shining up in beams of light from your toes. The brilliance is especially bright on the front of your legs. It spirals along your trunk and concentrates between your navel and your chest. A more celestial shade of gold pours from Saturn above and meets the earthy brass in your center. Feel a gentle warmth, the temperature just right, cradling you. Enjoy this sensation.

When you feel centered and supported, release the visualization.

CHAPTER 5

LISTENING TO THE MESSAGES OF YOUR BODY

The Earth element reminds us that we must practice and concretize our highest ideals. As the meeting place of matter and spirit, the body is an altar and activation portal. Consider that the body could be a wisdom keeper supporting your consciousness during this human experience. This chapter invites you to pay attention to your body's wisdom and focus on tangible actions toward the world you desire.

The idea of "mind over matter" positions the intellect as superior to and separate from our physical selves. The Chinese medical perspective, by contrast, locates spiritual, emotional, and mental energies within the trunk of the body. The five Yin organs are home to the Five Spirits 五神 of the Ethereal Soul, Heart Spirit, Intellect, Corporeal Soul, and Willpower. Through pulse diagnosis, a Chinese medical practitioner can assess the harmony of the patient's Five Elements in terms of physical as well as emotional and spiritual health. For centuries, Chinese physicians thought that the brain was a "sea of marrow," connected to the bones and the Water element. Rather than the mind being a dictator reigning from the skull, the Intellect 意 lives in the very center with the Earth element. The brain-gut-microbiome observed by biomedical researchers confirms the relationship between the central nervous system and bacteria in the digestive system.

ATTUNEMENT EXERCISE

1. What does my baseline physical equilibrium feel like? Taste like? Smell like? Look like? Sound like? What does my body experience in a healthy equilibrium? What sensations are green light messages that indicate all is well?

2. How do my senses inform me that my boundaries have been crossed? What do I experience physically, emotionally, and spiritually in these moments? What sensations are yellow light messages that indicate I may need to set a boundary, reach out, and/or modify my behavior?

3. How do my senses inform me that a group dynamic has become harmful? What do I experience physically, emotionally, and spiritually in these moments? What sensations are red light messages that indicate I may need to leave a situation or take more serious action?

4. How might I have suppressed or ignored these embodied messages?

5. What people and institutions benefit when I ignore my intuitive knowledge?

You might not be trained in pulse diagnosis, but you are the first point of contact for the messages of your Five Spirits. Physical symptoms and sensations are full of information from your soma and psyche that the conscious mind may not know. When you approach physical and emotional responses as communication from knowledgeable entities within you, the body becomes a wise ally.

INTERNAL WARNING SYSTEM

The body is constantly communicating, but we often miss its messages. To meet deadlines, make rent, and pay the bills, most of us have learned to ignore the ways our bodies talk to us. It takes deliberate attention to relearn the subtle signals of our intuition and embodied senses.

SENSE OF TOUCH

In this world of screens where your field of vision is prime real estate for marketers, closing your eyes can be healing. The more time you can spend in still contemplation, the easier it becomes to perceive and interpret the body's communication. Unblocking the body's rivers of Qi can also help.

Qigong and taijiquan, internal forms of gentle movement (as opposed to external martial arts like kung fu), open meridians for improved sensation. Forming your hands into soft, loose fists, tap below your navel across to your left hip. Ascending the side body to the armpit, tap in the axillary fold to awaken the lymph stored there. Descending back to your left hip, return to the center line and ascend toward your chest, staying right below your clavicle for about fifteen taps to stimulate the thymus. Let your right hand tap around the breast and up to the shoulder, then down the outside of the arm (the part that gets tan in summertime). When you reach the back of the hand, flip to the palm and tap up the inner aspect of the arm.

Shake out your arm as you relax from shoulder to pinky finger. Repeat on the right side.

Reaching behind you, tap softly on your lower back. If it feels good—don't strain yourself—tap down past the gluteal muscles and along the back of your legs to the feet. Then tap up along the inside of the legs to the pelvis. Take some time to break up stagnation right at the crease where the legs meet the trunk. Mirroring the armpits, this location is home to lymph glands and can become blocked when a person sits most of the day. Be very delicate here, because it's an area of the body where many people experience consent violations.

After unblocking the meridians of the body, brush yourself off as if removing dust. In the center of the palms, all of us have the Palace of Labor 勞宮, a special "ghost point" with both clinical and esoteric applications. Breathing in and out with attention at this point is a qigong practice that amplifies your healing abilities. Many cultures practice healing through the hands, and it works. With a soft palm, wipe off all areas of your body where you want to remove energies you do not need.

Returning to stillness, you might close your eyes. Without visual stimulation, you can drop into greater awareness of your physical form. Where inside or on the surface of your body do you sense pleasure? Sensitivity? Openness? Blockage? Agitation? Stillness? Is there any intuitive response your body tells you would help to soothe you? Do any images appear to communicate a message? Perceive proprioception at work, the muscles of your body sensing your physical position, motion, and surroundings. Also called kinesthesia, this state of receptivity orients you in space even with your eyes closed. As thoughts arise and fall, become aware of yourself as the witness. This contemplative state is an ancient Daoist practice called Chan, which is also fundamental to Zen meditation. From a Daoist perspective, it can be a way to connect with the undifferentiated source 無極.

It's essential to acknowledge that contemplative practices are not a panacea that work for everyone, and they can result in harmful outcomes for trauma survivors. Sitting in stillness might be overwhelming for someone whose body is holding the memory of violation. There is positive quantitative and qualitative research on meditation, but neuroscientist Catherine Kerr cautions against jumping to conclusions that mindfulness is a cure-all. Popular media outlets often extrapolate far beyond what a single study concludes. As someone who survived a traumatic experience in a Buddhist monastery, I know that mindfulness (like most practices) can hurt some people and in certain situations. Cheetah House is a nonprofit dedicated to supporting meditators in distress, who often feel isolated and ashamed to admit that the mat has been a site of suffering rather than enlightenment.

Attunement to your sense of touch should first and foremost be about your own desires and needs. Whether you want to dance wildly or wiggle your toes in the grass, jump into ocean waves or sunbathe on the sand, I want you to give yourself the sensations your body needs. If you aren't crossing other people's boundaries in the name of your yearning, there is nothing wrong with following your longings. If you were taught to fear or hate your own desires, this could take time, and you deserve all the time you need. Reading Audre Lorde's *Uses of the Erotic: The Erotic as Power* can support you in healing your relationship to pleasure.

Pushing back on the idea that the body's desires are sinful, harm reduction theory is another tool to shift your relationship to craving and need. Harm reduction is an alternative to pathologizing people who use drugs and other substances or behaviors. Clinical research clearly shows the connection between adverse childhood experiences (ACEs) and addiction later in life, which means that many people who use substances are survivors. Coping mechanisms that cause harm also serve a purpose, such as managing overwhelming pain. Whether or not your self-regulation strategies are as stigmatized as addiction, shifting to an attitude of humility and curiosity is an alternative to judgment. Spending hours watching reality TV while eating ice cream, from a Chinese medical perspective, could be the body's attempt to regulate Fire and Earth elements. Laughter is the emotion of Fire, which balances excess Metal in the form of grief. Procrastinating on work to watch comedy might indicate that sorrow needs tending. The sweet flavor corresponds to the Earth element, and might be an unconscious effort to tonify Spleen Qi if that energy is exhausted from intellectual activity. Harm reduction emphasizes meeting needs in safer ways as opposed to total abstinence, so in this example one might try to substitute fruit or honey if the desire persists after a bowl of ice cream.

LISTENING VERSUS OBEYING

For millennia, acupuncturists have been primary care physicians who seek to prevent illness before it worsens. Rather than a boutique commodity priced at more than $100 per session, Chinese medicine through the ages was for everyday people. The community acupuncture movement seeks to make this medicine accessible again so that ordinary people can afford to see their acupuncturist regularly. In weekly or more frequent sessions, a practitioner ideally has time to interpret the information the body is communicating before pathological progression.

The more we ignore the body's messages, the more our physiological problems escalate. A delay in getting to the emergency room can be a life-and-death situation for someone during an ectopic pregnancy or cardiac arrest. It is profoundly unjust that many people cannot afford the preventive medical care they need and must override pain to stay employed and avoid eviction. While this chapter encourages readers to pay attention to the body, it's essential that I recognize that doing so is a luxury.

To the extent that it is feasible in your situation, I invite you to attune to the difference between listening to and obeying the body. Acknowledging an impulse or feeling is not the same as immediately reacting, but this is particularly challenging in the context of trauma. Trauma survivors can physiologically be stuck in an acute stress response, the limbic system springing into action and taking the reins from conscious thought. In the presence of a perceived threat, the hypothalamus triggers a reaction that goes straight to the amygdala before the prefrontal cortex processes the information. As best you can, observe your instinctive attempts to remedy discomfort, then consider how you can meet your needs in the most loving way possible. As you might kneel to a small child who's tugging on your sleeve, try to give sensations caring attention. You may or may not do what the child wants, but you can validate what they're feeling and thank them for feeling safe enough to share with you.

When our bodies are activated into survival mode, it's much easier to enact harm upon ourselves and others. Contemporary existence and the systemic oppression that often animates it is traumatic. Trauma interrupts our ability to perceive reality and respond from our conscious integrity. Those who benefit from structural oppression must develop their capacity to receive constructive feedback (especially when it's not "nice") without spiraling. For oppressed people, choosing to prioritize the body's needs instead of its productivity is a revolutionary act. Since most of us experience both privilege and some form of marginalization, this requires courageous honesty and compassion. It requires ongoing embodied practice.

REALITY CHECKS

When the limbic system rushes into action, it can be helpful to physically soothe your entire body. Starting from the crown of your head, bring attention to sensation. Descending, see if you can relax your forehead and jaw. Open and close your eyes a few times, raise and lower your eyebrows, and open and shut your mouth. To open the Bright Yang 陽明 channels that run through the face, you can squeeze your facial muscles tight as if you've tasted something sour, then release the tightness on an exhale. Making silly expressions can also get Qi moving more freely in this area. Let gravity pull your head down gently, and allow it to roll from shoulder to shoulder. (I do not recommend rolling the head back, eyes facing up, because this can put pressure on the cervical vertebrae and many important nerves.) Breathe into your neck muscles with gratitude for all they do: the head is one of the heaviest parts of the body. Lift and drop your shoulders, tightening upward on the inhale and releasing on the exhale. Keeping your fingers together, grasp the tissue between your neck and shoulder, pulling upward with your fingers and thumb. This pinching-grasping movement of Chinese massage 推拿 Tuīná is best applied with gentle-strong-gentle pressure, beginning and ending with softness. You can rub this area with your palm afterward to soothe any blood flow. Using the same hand position, squeeze down each arm. Roll your shoulders backward and forward, windmill your elbows, and twirl your wrists. Shake out your hands like you've just washed them and there are no paper towels.

Attention to the trunk of the body is a way to soothe the Five Spirits in the organs. Try moving your sternum forward and backward off your center as if it's being pulled by a magnet. Let your rib cage pull you from side to side, then try to circle your chest while keeping your pelvis in the same place. With your hands on your hips, lean back as far as possible and notice your chest opening toward the sky. Envision golden light floating down to illuminate your center. Leaning forward, feel openness between your scapulae as if wings are sprouting.

Keeping your hands on your hips, begin to make gentle circles, an equal number in each direction. Lowering your hands to your knees, bend and straighten your legs a few times. Circling them in both directions, press gently from above the kneecap and imagine synovial fluid lubricating the joint. Tighten and release your calf and thigh muscles. Steadying yourself with a hand if needed, rotate your ankles one by one. Point and relax your feet, then shake out each leg. Keeping your knees soft, bounce up and down with the level of vigor that you feel you need. You can fortify this motion with the intention of breaking stagnation, increasing blood flow and oxygenation throughout the body, supporting the lymphatic and endocrine systems, and externalizing stress. Slowly reduce the tempo of your bouncing until you are almost still, keeping your knees soft. Close your eyes and observe the sensations you feel from head to toe and note any changes. Feel the subtle shifts that your body makes to balance you, even in stillness. See if you can draw your inhale down to the lower abdomen and lengthen the duration of your exhale.

Once your breathing has slowed down, you might put everything on paper. It can help to write down all your thoughts and feelings, uncensored, in bullet-point form. If this brings up a physical response, you can return to the grounding exercise above.

Next, try to distinguish feelings from facts. This is not to discount the importance of emotions, but to allow you to respond to present conditions as opposed to unresolved events from the past. I sometimes circle the facts, color-code them, and rewrite them in a different sequence of bullet points.

The facts help us discern an appropriate response to the situation at hand. The feelings that come with them are messengers that may tell us we need to set a boundary, make a change, or revisit issues we might have thought resolved.

After these preliminary steps, it can help to reach out to trustworthy people. Some friends and chosen family are highly emotionally intelligent and can help with working through feelings. Others have a gift for rational problem-solving, and they might be the ones to turn to for help brainstorming a response to a situation.

The wisdom and healing power of all five elements are present in our communities. Friends with strengths of the Wood element could cheer you on before you act and encourage you to follow through. Someone with strong Fire energy might support you in finding joy after disappointment. A friend with Metal energy could help make sense of complex information and organize a response. For a cosmic perspective, you might want to turn to a Water friend. A friend with great compassion and nurturing qualities could be a grounding Earth presence in your support system.

LISTENING PRACTICES

One strategy to harmonize the Intellect 意 and the body is to reflect on your physical sensations in a journal or sketchbook. You may draw three columns with the following headings: "What was happening?" "How was my body responding?" "What message was my body communicating?" Recording your physical reactions and reflecting upon them can reveal patterns. You might discover unresolved issues from childhood or past generations of your family. The data you gather can hone your intuition and help you pick up on subtle dynamics that your conscious mind missed. This resource might be private, or you could share your findings with someone you trust. Let the practice deepen your intimacy with and respect for your body.

ELEMENTAL COMMUNITY EXERCISE

1. Who makes me laugh and keeps me from taking myself too seriously? Who helps me cheer up and find joy? These people have Fire medicine.

2. Who has the gift of compassion, holding space, and providing comfort? These nurturing folks have Earth medicine. Do I reciprocate their care in a balanced exchange?

3. Who thinks systematically and adapts easily to change? Who perceives with clarity and justice? Who analyzes data into clear recommendations? This is Metal medicine.

4. Who brings wisdom to contemporary problems? Who ponders deeply and models determination to persevere? These people provide Water medicine.

5. Who breaks me out of a funk and inspires me to act? Who gets angry on my behalf if I'm being mistreated? Who courageously begins, pushing past procrastination? This is Wood medicine.

CHAPTER 6

WEEDING

In this chapter, we'll work at the intersection of Wood and Earth. Invasive species are an example of Wood overacting on Earth, a common Chinese medical diagnosis that can be understood as anger and eagerness (Wood) creating an imbalance in nourishing stability (Earth). Rosebud 玫瑰花 enters both Wood and Earth meridians, so you might want to have some rosebud tea while you read this chapter. Acupuncturists often diagnose indigestion as the by-product of Wood-Earth disharmony. When too much active plant energy is disturbing the soil, it's time to practice weeding.

The land now called California is home to Indigenous nations who preserved the biosphere for millennia. For generations, native people practiced controlled burns that prevented buildup of dry vegetation. Excess Wood not only weakens the Earth element but also leads the Fire element into excess through the generating cycle. Reducing Wood is essential for Earth to recuperate and Fire to return to a warm hearth light, not a blaze. This metaphysical interpretation respects all elements as inherently natural and neutral, merely out of balance. An invasive species in one ecosystem is indigenous in its home. When in proportion, Wood energy aerates the soil and, through the Amazon rain forest, oxygenates our planet.

A Chinese proverb advises "Destroy the roots when you pull up the weed." Another proverb states "To see the vista, one must climb the mountain." To create societies that practice reciprocal relationship with all of nature will take phenomenal, collaborative effort—far harder than ascending Mount Everest. Putting in the time and withstanding the difficulties of uprooting injustice is necessary for our species to restore equilibrium in the biosphere.

The exercises that follow are opportunities to get at the root, which is the definition of radical. Going slowly can help you identify the thinner, deeper tendrils of roots that can break off if you rush to pull out a weed too soon. Counter Wood element's aggressive impatience with the patience of Earth.

LAND CONNECTION EXERCISE

1. How does your body remember the land your people are indigenous to? For example, if you come from mountains, perhaps you are short in stature and can breathe at high altitudes. Are there physical traits that dominant society sees as ugly that in fact are assets in your homeland?

2. If you are no longer living on your ancestors' homelands, how might you reconnect (in ways that are respectful to those who never left)? Dancing to traditional music, cooking favorite dishes, or celebrating holidays can evoke the energy of home.

WEEDING

In the ecosystem of your own being, you are the sovereign steward of both the tangible and intangible. The late teacher Thich Nhat Hanh said to "walk as if you are kissing the Earth with your feet." Can you tread lightly and reverently, honoring the sacred below you as well as within you?

HARMONIZATION EXERCISE

1. Remove your shoes to apply acupressure to your big toes. Using your finger or a crystal, massage the skin right near the lower corners of each big toenail. This activates both the Yin Earth and Yin Wood meridians through the points Hidden White 隱白 and Big Mound 大敦.

2. Face the east and, if possible, find a green pen and/or piece of paper. Use them to write responses to the following questions:

   a. What stories about who I am and what I am capable of did I hear growing up?

   b. Do these feel true?

   c. What else might be possible? Who did I say I was when I was a child?

   d. What beliefs and behaviors are foreign and harmful to me?

3. Carry your answers outside your home and to a recycling bin. Envision a friendly green dragon coming to take them away.

4. Uncap the ends of your fingers and toes by gently tugging with intent. Imagine a dirty, decayed shade of green draining out into the soil, where it transforms into a cheerful sunflower yellow.

5. Place the palms of your hands on your belly, equidistant from your navel and the base of your sternum (where your ribs separate). Feel golden light rising from the soles of your feet and up to your core, gathering behind your hands and swirling in a globe of brightness.

6. In your mind's eye, notice if there are any remaining "weeds" and use your intent to carefully extract them. You may use your fingers to pluck or twist to the left, then shake out your hands to send the energy into the earth. Notice sensations of spaciousness and relaxation with each invasive plant you remove.

7. The golden radiance fills you up and shields you. You can return to this exercise periodically and notice if psychic weeds return in similar areas of your energy body. If so, go even slower and deeper to find their roots.

Equilibrium Visualization

Close your eyes and bring attention to the points of contact that connect you to the earth. Feel the support that is holding you up without inhibiting free movement. At the base of the ball of each foot, envision a cork popping open, allowing golden-yellow roots to extend from your feet into the center of the Earth. Boundless strength, nourishment, care, and aid begin to flow up your legs toward the sky. You become aware that your core is a trunk, your arms are branches, and above the crown of your head extend twigs reaching for sunlight. Feel the symmetry between your root system below the soil and your boughs opening toward the heavens. Earth's consistent presence is the foundation for the iridescent emerald leaves budding all around you. Contrasted by the vigorous outward motion of your plant energy, Earth is still, making it possible for Wood to move.

In the center of your trunk, you notice that buttercup-yellow light illuminates the hexagram Earth ☷ 坤 right above your Spleen and Stomach. Below your right breast, the hexagram for Wood ☴ 巽 shines from your Liver and Gallbladder. A Taijitu symbol appears between the two trigrams a deep goldenrod tone for Yin and pale green for Yang. Spiraling in harmony, green and yellow light radiate to the uppermost tips of your tree and down to the embedded roots. Flowers begin to blossom and then drop petals upon the ground. In their place, fruit ripens in jewel tones. Falling to the earth, the fruit joins the flowers in turning yellow. They merge into the ground as compost that regenerates the soil.

Feel within yourself an equilibrium of vitality and serenity, rest and enthusiasm. When you feel restored, open your eyes.

WEEDING EXERCISE

1. Research the native plants and invasive species in your area.

2. Use a plant identification app or pictures to literally weed out the invasive species if you have a garden or yard, adding the intention of weeding those qualities within yourself that are out of balance.

3. Notice how much attention is needed to pull out weeds from the root so they don't grow back.

4. Plant native species, especially those that feed pollinators. Even a windowsill plant is great.

5. If you don't have your own outdoor space, try to find a park or public natural area and practice identifying native plants. Say their traditional names if possible and thank them for their role in the ecosystem that is sustaining you. Know that the ancestors of the land stewards are buried in the soil, and the cells of native plants might once have been ancestors who walked the land.

Part Three

METAL

火

土

金

水

木

Alchemy

Organizes and contains

Creates tools and systems

Shifts shape and composition

Planet: Venus 金星 Jīn Xīng

Direction: West

Season: Autumn

Guardian: White Tiger of the West 西方白虎 Xī Fāng Bái Hǔ

Lunar mansions: Legs 奎 Kuí, Bond 婁 Lóu, Stomach 胃 Wèi, Hairy Head 昴 Mǎo, Net 畢 Bì, Turtle Beak 觜 Zī, Three Stars 參 Shen

Color: White

Emotion: Sorrow

Organs: Lung, Large Intestine

Spirit: Corporeal Soul 魄 Po

Trigrams: ☰ Heaven 乾 Qian, ☱ Lake 兌 Dui

Affirmation: I am clear and integrated.

CHAPTER 7

THE WHITE TIGER
OF THE WEST

To connect with the element Metal, face the west. It can be helpful to attune your Metal energy when you feel sad, when you need to set boundaries, or during autumn. Wearing white cloth and golden jewelry, you might envision a mirrored bubble reflecting away misfortune. Throughout your day, you can quietly shield yourself by envisioning white light from Venus gathering in your lungs, then enveloping you completely. On the western horizon, imagine a white tiger coming to life among the constellations and descending to walk with you as a protector.

The west is also the direction of the ancestors, where the sun sets after a long day. Sitting with your heart facing the west, you can speak aloud what you're ready to let go of—the Large Intestine is a Metal organ that teaches us to release what we no longer need. Allow yourself to cry if you need to, as each tear relieves your body of the stress hormone cortisol. If you were taught that crying is weak when you were growing up, I hope that you now have access to safe people who know that expressing emotion takes courage. A Chinese proverb goes "True gold does not fear fire." Tears may burn as they fall from our eyes, but you will not melt. You can be an ancestor who releases emotional repression from your family line.

BOUNDARIES AS SEMIPERMEABLE MEMBRANE

Our cells protect themselves with lipid membranes that are flexible but strong. These tiny microcosms of our being know how to allow in what is nourishing and externalize what they no longer need. Honoring our own boundaries prevents us from developing resentment when others defend theirs. Respecting our limits is a prerequisite for us to show up in relationships, which is where collective power lies.

The metaphor of a semipermeable membrane is important, because some exchange across barriers is necessary. While maintaining homeostasis within, cell membranes must allow nutrients in and waste products out. In the energetic space around and within us, we need to discern what serves us and what does not. Giving and receiving is sustainable when boundaries are clear but not hermetic. It can be tempting to deflect any less-than-flattering perspectives, but that moves us along the spectrum of selfishness toward narcissism. Sometimes constructive feedback is beneficial although unpleasant. Dismissing critique out of hand as "haters" being jealous is a dangerous precedent. A flexible, living boundary can absorb cruelty while allowing in calls for accountability. This dynamic membrane can even separate the two when they arrive mixed together, as is sometimes the case. You can refuse to allow vitriol within your energy field and still acknowledge the kernel of fact within the message. It is bitter medicine, but the alternative is losing integrity.

Pushback and manipulation are common reactions to boundaries, and they indicate the other person is not well. Even if you communicate what you can and cannot do with neutral clarity and compassion, people in pain may feel triggered and act out. Their feelings are not your responsibility. You can care about their suffering and perhaps lift them up in prayer, but ultimately each person is responsible for their own emotions.

We can co-regulate, a psychobiological term that refers to a set of behavior interventions that support another person or persons in calming their nervous system. Verbally acknowledging the other's distress, modeling deep breathing, and using a warm tone of voice are examples of co-regulation. It is not possible, however, to save someone from their own unpleasant emotional-physical sensations. To presume to have that power shows an unconscious arrogance, a sense of superiority within oneself and lack of capacity in the other.

In infant-caregiver situations and with young children, supportive adults attune with kids' physiological and emotional states, affirm that the relational attachment can sustain the child's distress, and help little ones in managing their responses. People who didn't receive this care during early life can struggle with complex PTSD and its effects on their bodies, including experiencing boundaries as abandonment.

Between adults, it is not appropriate to step into a parent-child dynamic, even while we acknowledge that the other person is dealing with childhood trauma. Know that someone who has an extreme reaction to a clear limit is probably reliving painful experiences, because trauma is time travel. They might be unconsciously trying to work through past relational rupture with you. With empathy, do your best to stay in the present moment. By honoring your own limits, you model for them how to set boundaries, which they may not have been permitted to hold. The flip side is that it's important to know when you're the one who's reacting to another's boundaries based on past trauma.

If there is truth in criticism you receive, it's a good idea to write it down and plan to act on the new knowledge. When we receive information that feels painful, the first order of business is to self-soothe and get grounded. Then, pay attention to the source. What power dynamics are at play? If I have structural advantages in relation to the person giving me feedback, I know that I need to consult with a trustworthy third party whose politics

I trust. Accountability buddies in the support team you develop later will assist you.

In the element Wood, you will identify the relationships that can be containers for this type of transformation. It's important to have people who will be kind, but not enable us. We need confidants who we know will be honest with us.

BOUNDARY EXERCISE

1. What messages did I internalize about boundaries growing up?

2. How does my body tell me that my boundaries are being crossed?

3. What are my physical boundaries?

4. What are my emotional boundaries?

5. What are my spiritual boundaries?

6. Whom do I trust to respect my boundaries?

7. How do I check in about others' boundaries?

8. How can I make amends when I cross others' boundaries?

9. How do I differentiate between a boundary violation and constructive feedback?

LETTING GO

To interrupt intergenerational patterns of harm, we need to be mindful not to allow internal or external sabotage to fester. As cycle-breakers, we are trying to clean house for future generations, not accumulate more junk. The Yang organ of the Metal element is the Large Intestine, which releases our waste material regularly. Spiritually, the Metal element supports us both in cleansing and protection. The immune system pertains to the Yin aspect of the Metal element, keeping pathogens out of our bodies by fighting threats and maintaining our boundaries. Metal supports us in externalizing what we do not need. We will begin with cleansing through release because detoxifying your energetic space makes it easier to fortify protective barriers.

RELEASING EXERCISE

1. How did I express emotion and release tension as a child?

2. When do I remember feeling light, free, and renewed? What led to that feeling? Are there any actions or practices I engaged in that I can return to?

3. Are there any releasing practices that older generations in my lineage have used? What about further back in time? Consider researching traditions of your known ancestors.

Here are some suggestions for letting go:

- Dancing the hokey pokey. The shaking of limbs is part of many qigong and taijiquan warm-ups!

- Writing or drawing in a free-flowing manner.

- Envisioning pure, cleansing rain washing over and through you.

- Defecating and urinating with the intent to cleanse and release spiritually.

- Vocalizing whatever sounds the body wants to make.

- Holding on to ethically sourced crystals and speaking what you want to release into the stones (regularly cleanse them with salt water).

- Exfoliating with a mixture of salt and honey.

- Deep-cleaning your space; scrubbing or sweeping vigorously.

- Exercising, especially aerobics and martial arts.

- Reflecting in a nightly journaling session:

  - What am I grateful for?

  - In what ways did I show up as a healing ancestor today?

  - What did I learn?

  - Do I need to course-correct?

  - What can I release?

Protection Visualization

Enter your practice space by grounding into your body. Consciously let your body become heavier, and allow gravity to pull any tension out of you into the earth below. Opalescent moonlight begins to gently shower down upon you, shimmering and sparkling as it cleanses you from crown to root.

Inhale deep into your core and allow yourself to release your exhale with any sound your body needs to make. On your next inhale, fill yourself with that iridescent moonlight, then exhale everything you no longer need. Once more, expand your lungs to receive abundant nourishing energy, then expel through your mouth with a sound of relief.

Now that you are glowing with moonlight, say your name three times. You notice you are within your sanctuary. What time of day is it? Is the sky full of stars? Rainbows? Sunbeams?

One of your guardians approaches you with a smile. Is this a sphinx? A dragon? A tiger? An angel? Pegasus? This being invites you to climb upon its back. Together, you fly into the celestial space above your sanctuary, and you realize that your sacred space is within your own heart.

From this perspective, you see your body as a beautiful galaxy full of life. Your protector flies with you above the landscape of hills, valleys, mountains, and seas that make up your wonderful physical being. Your skin is a sacred boundary that protects the delicate, intricate magic within. The skin teaches us that we can repair ruptures in our boundary system, that a wound can become a scab and then a scar that shows our resilience.

Your vantage point expands to perceive the sphere that surrounds your physical body, what some call the aura. With your guardian, you are going to strengthen this energetic boundary beyond the skin. Where in your aura are there ruptures or breakage? Your guardian flies to each point and repairs your aura. Does your protector use fire? Plasma? Starlight? Wood? Take your time. Your guardian is a powerful, benevolent immortal being who can call on magical energies to protect and support you. Tend to all tears in your energetic boundaries.

When you're ready, you fly together back to the sanctuary in your heart. The flickering firelight warms you, and your younger selves embrace you happily. You return to the mandala in the center of your sanctuary, breathe deep, and say your name three times. Gently return to your waking life with a wiggle of your toes.

EMBODIED PRACTICES

In Chinese medical theory, the Lung is the most exterior organ. Like an umbrella that shields the rest of the body, the Lung and the Metal element protect through the immune system and the skin. The progression of a mild cough to pneumonia exemplifies the role of the Lung as a first responder. Chinese herbs are phenomenally effective at preventing this kind of development. If you experience simultaneous sensations of warm and cold with an occipital headache, this can mean the Protective Qi is fighting an external pathogen. This warrior energy circulates at the surface of the body as the first line of defense, just like the skin functions as a physical barrier to prevent disease from entering. Moisturizing your skin while facing west is a simple, accessible method of energetic protection. As you nourish your largest organ, acknowledge the skin for keeping harmful things out and guarding what is precious. Notice light reflecting off the hydrated surface of your skin like armor.

Sound healing for the Metal element tonifies the organs and meridians. If you wake up before seven a.m., you can fortify this practice as Qi circulates through the Yang Metal meridian. Inhale into your lower abdomen, and then release while making the sound *ts*. The tongue touches the roof of the mouth right behind the front teeth as you form the shape of the joint consonants *t* and *s*. Visualize white light shining along the radial aspect of your hands and arms, coating your skin and covering your Lung and Large Intestine. Set the intention of fortifying your respiratory and immunological systems.

The Jing-Well point on the Lung channel can help with hot sore throat and emotional disturbance. Just beyond the lower corner of the thumbnail, on the inside of the hand, closer to the thumb than the pinky finger, Lesser Shang 少商 Shàoshāng revives unconsciousness. Acupuncturists use this point for painful throat obstruction and cough with emotional upset.

Kitchen herbalism for the Metal element is especially applicable during the autumn, but can be helpful all year long. Fall is a time to gather the dispersed energies of summer and conserve Qi for winter. Scallion 蔥白 supports Protective Qi in expelling external pathogens and is a highly effective folk remedy for the early stages of a cold. These green onions are best used if sensations of cold predominate, and they can be consumed with ginger tea to exacerbate the warming effect. Hua-Ching Ni recommends boiling a piece of garlic with brown sugar to treat a cold, as well. For a chronic dry cough with phlegm and sensations of cold, you can scrape out the seeds in an Asian pear and fill the cavity with fritillaria bulbs. Adding a little brown sugar makes for a sweet and nurturing remedy.

METAL SEASON FOODS

During Metal season, teacher and nutrition researcher Paul Pitchford recommends moderate use of sour foods like adzuki beans, rose hip tea, yogurt, salt plums, leeks, and cheese. Many mushrooms benefit the lungs, such as cordyceps 冬蟲夏草, "Turkey Tail" coriolus 雲芝, and reishi 靈芝. Foods that support the mucous membranes of the lungs include marshmallow root, fenugreek, flaxseed, and kelp 昆布 and other seaweeds. Chilis and spicy peppers can protect Lung health, and pungent white foods are especially beneficial. Turnip, garlic, horseradish, daikon radish, white peppercorn, and various types of onions aid in the dispersing action that the Metal element uses to expel pathogens and disseminate Qi throughout the body. Eating these foods raw exacerbates this action, while brief cooking is more appropriate if you feel low in energy.

CHAPTER 8

THROUGH THE LOOKING GLASS

The self-compassion of the element Fire and the supportive empowerment of the element Earth bring us to self-reflection with the element Metal. With Metal's discernment, clarity, and capacity for transformation, we will identify attitudes and behavior patterns in ourselves. The element Metal can change shape and form, and so can we. In the alchemical light of element Fire, Metal embodies the energy of change.

Self-doubt and self-hatred block spiritual growth and progress. This chapter is designed to cut away the projections of others and all forms of internalized supremacy or inferiority. In discerning human delusions from spiritual truth, you will rediscover the glory you have always been and always will be. Transforming your self-perception strengthens your ability to show up for life with spiritual strength.

As you move through the exercises that follow, keep coming back to your breathing. How fully can you exhale? What emotions show up? The emotion of the element Metal is grief, and all feelings need to flow. Can you breathe through what arises?

DAOIST PARABLE

Storytelling is one of the most ancient methods of teaching spiritual principles. The parable that follows is a traditional story that illustrates Metal element neutrality and perspective.

An elderly farmer cultivated her land for decades. There came a day that her horse ran away from the farm. When her village heard what had happened, her neighbors expressed their sympathy. "This is so unfortunate," they said.

"Maybe, maybe not," she answered.

The following day, the horse came back, accompanied by three wild horses.

"What good luck!" her neighbors rejoiced.

"Maybe, maybe not," the farmer replied.

Later that day, her son broke his leg trying to ride one of the wild horses. The villagers bemoaned her ill fortune. "Such bad luck," her neighbors cried.

"Maybe, maybe not," she told them.

The next morning, the farmer's village received military officials who demanded all young men report for armed service. Upon seeing the farmer's son was injured, they left without him. Her neighbors celebrated the lucky outcome.

"Maybe, maybe not," she softly replied, her eye to the North Star.

Try to be like the farmer as you consider the reflection you perceive in the element Metal's mirror.

VALUES

Before addressing what needs work, we need clarity of values. When unconsciously scrolling through social media, we are influenced by algorithms set by companies whose priorities might not match our own. In the exercise that follows, I invite you to use the power of intention to clarify your personal value system. Consciously defining your own moral compass is a path to self-respect and a sense of dignity.

VALUES EXERCISE

1. What qualities do you admire in the people you love most?

2. What traits did you admire in your primary caregivers? Do you still value those traits?

3. Who did you admire and emulate when you were growing up? What qualities did you aspire to? Have the people and characteristics you respect changed over time? If so, how?

4. What qualities do you aspire to in your spiritual and personal growth?

5. What are three ways you are already living your values?

6. What choices, patterns, or investments are out of alignment with these values?

   a. In the way you treat yourself?

   b. In the way you treat those close to you?

   c. In your public life?

7. Draw two columns and title one "Key Value" and the other "Why It Matters." Choose three to five key values that are especially meaningful for you.

You may notice that your gifts are directly linked to your challenges. Excellent attention to detail can relate to overwhelming anxiety in the presence of disorder. Perceiving that your difficulties are related to your strengths can be liberating. They are not fixed flaws, but aspects of you as a perfectly imperfect, whole human being.

As you consider what needs work in your character, stay in touch with your inner children and younger selves. Remind them that you love them unconditionally. Explain that continuous self-reflection and course correction are part of being humans of integrity, not any form of punishment.

All you are doing is noting what energy you would like to transform.

APPRECIATION

1. What do you appreciate, value, and love about yourself today? What aspects of the life you live do you cherish? What choices did you make that made you who you are and gave you this life?

2. What are your gifts, talents, and skills? If you feel unsure, ask people who love you.

3. Are there any "negative" characteristics that are the flip side of your strengths?

4. What familial, societal, and global factors have shaped your strengths and challenges?

The trigrams for the Metal element are ☰ Heaven 乾 and ☱ Lake 兌. Still bodies of water reflect the sky and served as mirrors for ancient people.

The skies above radiate cosmic light through the sun, moon, and stars. This next writing exercise focuses on reflection. As you gaze upon your character, imagine that you are gazing into a clear lake with the Drinking Gourd constellation shimmering behind you.

REPRESENTATION

1. What aspects of your identity are well represented in the world around you?

2. What parts of you long for greater kinship and visibility?

3. What messages of your superiority have you internalized? From what sources? Who benefits?

4. What messages of your inferiority have you internalized? From what sources? Who benefits?

5. What habits and actions reinforce these dynamics of supremacy and inferiority in your life?

ON HUMILITY

Societies built on conquest valorize arrogance. Donald Trump rose to power because millions of people admired his selfish, egotistical behavior. He is not an anomaly but a product of his culture. In a culture that rewards cruelty with television shows and talk show appearances, humility is equated with humiliation. In fact, the person who cannot or will not admit their human frailty is profoundly insecure. Making mistakes is inevitable, but it is not a reason for shame unless one chooses not to learn.

Taking accountability and being willing to share power is not submission. The quest to be the best, number one, and the most powerful is patriarchal, imperial, and narcissistic.

Many Daoist sages preferred to be unnoticeable. Despite records of flight, multicentury longevity, and other miracles, these teachers chose simplicity and anonymity. The classic Daoist text *Daodejing* states that the hallmark of a great leader is when the leader's followers say they did the great task themselves.

Accepting our limitations is key to avoiding savior behavior and the inevitable burnout that follows. While we are alive, we will always fall short of our highest ideals, but we can keep coming back to the practice. By apologizing and making real amends, we can stay in relationships long enough to do meaningful work in the world. Humility is the mark of a person of inner strength, someone who is not dependent on external validation, someone whose value-centered core anchors their conduct. Without groveling in shame or posturing in arrogance, humble people gather the Qi of their Five Spirits within.

Humility is soul medicine.

INTERPERSONAL ROLES

Learning how to celebrate all the small victories that are part of the long game can prevent burnout. It is in this spirit that you will focus on what's working.

In your journal, mark two columns with the headings "What's working" and "What needs work." Turning the mirror inward on your conduct and beliefs, gently reflect on your alignment with your values. Try to feel the neutral clarity of the Metal element as you practice humility.

Dysfunctional dynamics are obstacles to a practice of humility. Psychiatrist Stephen Karpman used geometry to visualize one particularly destructive pattern that traps people in three roles, all of which deny us our full humanity. The "drama triangle" consists of the persecutor, rescuer, and victim. From these three positions, participants engage in various destructive behaviors that result in relational harm. When one person acts from the rescuer or victim position (I haven't observed many people self-identify as the villain), it can be challenging for others not to enter the resulting interpersonal "game." The victim role is disempowering, denying the individual's agency. The rescuer role quickly leads to resentment and manipulation due to a sense of martyrdom. When the victim deems the appointed rescuer insufficiently benevolent—which is inevitable because no human can save another—the victim often slides the rescuer into the role of persecutor. This dynamic may play out in families affected by addiction or trauma. While you cannot control whether others enter the drama triangle, your awareness of it can help you manage your own participation in its chaos.

DISCERNMENT EXERCISE

1. What roles do you tend to play in your relationships?

    a. Platonic

    b. Professional

    c. Familial

    d. Romantic

2. Do these roles feel aligned with who you came here to be?

Reclaim Your Narrative

Metal energy gives us tools to shape this human experience. In the following exercise, language will be your tool. As you consider the reflection of your character, remember that you are perceiving a snapshot of dynamic processes. Try to release the idea that you (or any of us) are fixed as a hero or villain. We are all on a tiny rock careening through a universe that we barely understand. Daoism teaches that transformation and change is the way of the cosmos. The information you gather through honest self-reflection is nothing more than a snapshot. Within you, matter and energy are constantly transforming through Yin and Yang, the Five Elements, and all the processes of the macrocosm that surrounds you. As much as every one of us, you deserve to be a work in progress.

SOUL SOVEREIGNTY

The phrase *soul sovereignty* is an invitation to practice reverence and responsibility with ourselves and others. Reading these words is a call for your consciousness to begin (or, most likely, continue) to actively acknowledge your indwelling divinity and consistently reflect on the alignment between your choices and your intentions.

The mirror of your character reflects source energy 無極, the undifferentiated origin or the 道 Dao. The body that carries your consciousness is a wonderful friend of your being, your lifelong companion and guardian, and its external appearance demonstrates only the resilience of your ancestors and the experience you have gained during this incarnation. Rather than focusing on external appearance, Daoists seek to become people of developed character 真人 whose conduct meets high ethical standards. By focusing on beautifying your inner qualities, you refine your energy and grow closer to your source.

Reverence for source energy within you involves care for your younger selves, which we worked on in our exploration of the element Fire; empowerment via tools to act with integrity, which we emphasized in our exploration of the element Earth; and appreciation for all that you are, which we focused on in our exploration of the element Metal. The responsibility to the source energy within you is an ongoing practice of mirror work as you pay attention to the relationship between intent and impact.

BIOGRAPHY EXERCISE

After reflecting on the projections of others and analyzing the facts of who you are, you will take up your pen as an author. Write your story from the third-person perspective of an unconditionally loving narrator. With as much generosity as possible, describe the path you've traversed in this lifetime. Honor your context and the hardships others didn't know about, and don't shy away from admitting errors. If it's hard to have compassion for yourself and to be honest about mistakes, take a deep breath and place your palms on your thighs. Return when you feel ready.

CHAPTER 9

INDWELLING DIVINITY, LIVING SUNLIGHT

In this chapter, you will honor the light within you and alchemize sorrow. In countering negativity bias that can lead to the Metal emotion of sorrow, we will be directing attention to all that is wonderful about you. We will celebrate the choices you've made, habits you've developed, and commitments you've maintained that make the world a more just, loving place for us all to live. In the controlling cycle of the Five Elements, Fire transforms Metal when it is in excess. This is the magic of the blacksmith's forge. Elementally, fire gives light, which dazzles when reflected in metal. By dancing in the metaphysical exchange of Metal element's Yin with Fire element's Yang, grief can become less intractable.

This relationship between Fire and Metal is not for spiritual bypassing. While most of us prefer joy to sorrow, the uplifting Fire energy of delight is not better or more important than Metal's heavy grief. Both live in the chest, where they create what Giovanni Maciocia calls Ancestral Qi. The Yin organs of Fire and Metal are the Heart and Lungs, respectively. Our physical hearts are cradled by our lungs, the flame of Fire surrounded in a lantern crafted of metal. Together, the heart and lungs oxygenate our blood and animate our lives. As you read this chapter, pay attention to your chest. Notice the rhythms of both your heartbeat and your breath playing in harmony.

FALLING LEAVES

The season of the Metal element is autumn, when plant kindred release the leaves that once drank sunlight. The element Metal gives us grief, bitter medicine that shows us what we love when we've lost it, and reminds us to let go. Weeping affects our breathing through the Yin Metal organ of the Lungs. Defecation via the Yang Metal Large Intestine relieves us of what we no longer need. Grief and surrender are some of the most challenging aspects of the human condition, and they were everywhere during the years 2020 and 2021: both Metal years in the Daoist calendar. The pain of Metal emotions is not meant to last forever, but to give way to Water and be balanced by Fire. We will face them in order to allow the process of change to move through us.

Metal energy organizes and creates systems. By intentionally creating space to feel grief in a safe container, we can distill the lessons sadness might be teaching us. This is best done in the hours of the Fire element, eleven a.m. to three p.m. or seven to eleven p.m.

Gaze at your inner mirror to discern what kind of support you need to do grief work. Survivors and those who are living with generational trauma may be carrying more pain than it is safe or realistic to process alone. If this is the case for you, I support you in reaching out to be held in your sorrow. Death and loss, as much as birth and connection, are reasons to gather with others. Although societal pressures urge us to suppress and push past sadness, you and your communities can choose to prioritize releasing the weight. Being held in someone's arms as you weep freely can be all you need.

GRIEF EXERCISE

1. Find a setting where you feel as supported and safe as possible.

2. Start a timer for five minutes. Face the west. On a white piece of paper, draw a representation of the people, places, and things you grieve having lost. Don't judge or edit what comes up for artistic quality or rationality. Allow yourself to externalize without internal critique.

3. When the timer goes off, reset it for another five minutes. Move to face the south, and hold your arms out in front of you, palms facing your chest. Let your fingers be loose but awakened, your hands extending from the wrists, not drooping. Flex and release your fingers a few times and see if you notice a tingling sensation or warmth in the center of your palms. Let your elbows and shoulders drop, leaving space for an egg between your upper arm and torso. Envision rose-gold light suffusing your heart and pouring down your arms into the center of the palms. There, it beams back into your heart. Stay with this visualization as you breathe naturally.

4. Repeat steps 2 and 3 five times, or until you feel complete.

5. Bring your drawing materials to face the south. While fully acknowledging sorrow's truth, connect to gratitude by drawing your experiences of joy, meaning, and unconditional love. Strengthen the connection to Fire by using paper or a writing utensil that is pink or red. Feel into the paradoxical human experience—is there any way that loss itself might make joy more sacred, deeper, and richer? Fire is the energy of love and joy. Does its warmth shift any of the sorrow?

6. When you feel ready, rub your palms together to generate heat. When your hands are warm, brush off your body as if removing dust. Envisioning rose-gold light glowing in the center of your palms, place your hands gently wherever you feel discomfort. Strengthen the motion with the intention of transforming pain and allowing space for joy.

Heart Release Ritual

Fire corresponds to joy and Metal to sorrow; in this ritual, readers will acknowledge both emotions as teachers that work together to alchemize experience into wisdom.

1. *Close your eyes and feel into your heart space, where rose-colored light shines with the joy and compassion of Fire.*

2. *When you feel deeply connected to the love in your heart, write down what habits and beliefs you would like to release like the leaves of autumn. Take a piece of paper (or better yet, a set of multicolored Post-it Notes) and write out those behaviors and attitudes you would like to release as leaves fall in the forest.*

3. *For each one, say thank you for the ways it has helped you get to where you are today.*

4. *Arrange your rainbow of Post-its and see if you can perceive the beauty of a forest floor in autumn.*

5. *Mindfully recycle your paper.*

MIRROR WORK

Amid a visual culture where celebrity and conspicuous consumption take center stage, I invite you to look into your inner mirror. This lesson is about noticing and celebrating the beauty within. On a spiritual level, the element Metal reflects your behaviors and actions, not your external appearance. What we give our attention to grows.

Polish your inner mirror each day by writing down at least three ways you brought more joy and love into the world. Speaking them aloud and thanking yourself can help reinforce that your choices are more important than your looks. Throughout your day, try to notice yourself acting in ways that seed liberatory, equitable futures, and pat yourself on the back—literally or figuratively. Contemplate what rewards you most anticipated in childhood and affirm yourself in the ways that feel best.

Whenever you receive a genuine compliment, practice taking a deep breath and letting it into your heart space. If it's written, take a photo. If it's virtual, take a screenshot. Create a digital photo album that consists of kind words. Whenever you receive constructive feedback, this archive of your glory is a file of evidence to counter shame's narrative that your mistakes define you.

APPRECIATION EXERCISE

1. Make a living list of choices you've made that brought more justice and love into the world.

2. Make a living list of your gifts, talents, and skill sets. Write a letter of admiration and appreciation to yourself. Read it aloud at regular intervals and/or record it.

Restoration Visualization

Release tension out of the soles of your feet, and draw your attention to gravity's gentle embrace. A pleasant tingling at the crown of your head flows down and through your being, and clear moonlight rejuvenates you with celestial energy. As you intentionally allow your muscles to relax, take three deep breaths. Each exhale removes carbon dioxide as well as sorrow. Saying your name three times, you emerge in your sacred grove.

From the west, you notice a shimmer. Moving toward it, you find a smooth mirror of crystal and gold. Instead of your physical form, it reflects a bright metallic light. In the heart of the light begin to appear images of moments when you acted with integrity. From your earliest memories to the present moment, you observe your character. The mirror demonstrates times when no one was there to witness, and you chose to do what was most courageous. Take time to remember.

After you have taken in this record of your legacy, you feel lighter. Let any tears fall that need to fall.

As weightless as a beam of light, you turn to the south and see a rosy radiance beckoning you. In the sky above, stars form the shape of a phoenix. Rose-gold luminescence pours down from the constellations and centers in your heart. You see your lungs glowing silver-white and your heart a sweet shade of ruby. From your lungs, the white light spreads to your skin and illuminates every pore. Your cardiovascular system gleams coral as it transmits oxygenated blood from head to toe. Laughter unfurls from your chest as you open into joy.

When you feel restored, return to the center of your sacred grove and say your name three times, breathing fresh air in a few deep inhales.

INVOCATION EXERCISE

1. Write an invocation to the best of who you are and can be.

    • First, write it in the past tense. Imagine the legacy you will leave behind at the end of this lifetime.

    • Next, write it in the present tense. "I am" is a potent manifestation phrase in and of itself. Read this aloud to yourself in front of your altar to yourself, perhaps on the new moon.

    • Review the values you discerned for yourself. Identify specific, measurable habits that align your actions with those principles.

    • Choose one habit per moon cycle. Begin with the new moon by writing down the value you chose and how the habit operationalizes your values.

    • Ask a supportive friend to be your accountability buddy.

    • Reward yourself on the full moon for persisting toward your new habit.

Part Four

WATER

火

土

金

水

木

Ancestral Inventory

The origin of our life force

Profound connection to Source

Enduring ancestral wisdom

Generative, adaptable, resilient

Planet: Mercury 水星 Shǔ Xīng

Direction: North

Season: Winter

Guardian: Mysterious Warrior 北方玄武 Běi Fāng Xuán Wǔ

Lunar mansions: Southern Dipper 斗 Dǒu, Ox 牛 Niú, Girl 女 Nǔ, Emptiness 虛 Xū, Rooftop 危 Wēi, Encampment 室 Shì, Wall 壁 Bì

Color: Blue or Black

Emotion: Fear

Organs: Kidney, Urinary Bladder

Spirit: Willpower 志 Zhì

Trigram: ☵ Water 坎 Kǎn

Affirmation: I am rooted and dignified.

CHAPTER 10

FUTURE ANCESTOR

To connect with the Water element, face the north. In the heavens, planetary elder Mercury is a source of Water energy that you can call on for cleansing blue-ebony light. In the body, Water organs are the Kidney and Urinary Bladder. You can place your hands on your lower back and breathe that energy deep into that area, feeling strength and support fill the well within you. During adversity, the element Water is the source of the Willpower 志 Zhi that can carry you through. Willpower is the spirit that endures harsh winter, the season of Water. The Mysterious Warrior is a wise and ancient tortoise, slow and resilient. Tortoises conserve energy by moving at a sustainable pace, resting when needed, and protecting the soft within firm boundaries. Notice and celebrate these qualities in yourself as you proceed through this section.

By diving into the depths of your lineage, you are certain to discover exquisite beauty as well as profound suffering. As a living emissary of your ancestors, you will take inventory of the stories, memories, beliefs, patterns, and traumas that you inherited. With the fluidity of the element Water, you will cleanse and clear what is no longer needed. Refreshed and wiser, you will move forward into action feeling rooted and dignified.

Hurt people hurt people, and the coping mechanisms of our ancestors may have twisted family systems into dysfunctional shapes. Working with intergenerational trauma is courageous, but not necessarily comfortable. In facing difficult truths about your ancestry or taking inventory of your privileges, you might feel overwhelmed.

When fear expresses itself in your body, take a moment to discern what it is communicating. If fear arises during the chapters that follow, practice curiosity about its origin. Human beings often do terrible things when we are afraid. If you are brave enough to admit fear, it means you are courageous. I invite you to pause, discern whether there is actual danger present, and feel deep into your bravery. If you are not, in fact, in any danger, Willpower 志 is a wellspring of strength to persevere. A Chinese proverb teaches that water droplets can penetrate stone.

ANCESTRAL COMMUNION

When eating fruit, recall the fruit tree; when drinking water, remember its source. 落其實者思其樹，飲其流者懷其源. In the element Water, you acknowledge yourself as the embodiment of myriad generations now gone.

In this book, you will move from research into application. By taking up the mantle of lineage bearer, you have a role in preserving and passing forward memories and practices that support your family line in being a presence of integrity on this planet. Please remember that your thriving joy is an offering of healing to all the ancestors who have gone before you.

Here are some suggestions to remember your source and unblock the channel of ancestral connection:

- Seek out videos of traditional dances and ceremonies your ancestors participated in.

- Find communities of practice that teach traditional dances, music, and spirituality.

- Make playlists of traditional music that your ancestors may have listened to, as well as songs that remind you of relatives with whom you have supportive relationships.

- Depict your family tree artistically.

- Interview family elders, taking notes and/or recording if they consent.

- Research the traditional clothing, jewelry, and adornments of your ancestors. If feasible, set aside a monthly budget to purchase pieces for your body and/or ancestor altar.

EPIGENETICS

Mitochondrial and nuclear DNA transmit genetic information across space-time. These braids of sugars and phosphate groups conjure great-great-grandmothers' cheekbones from centuries ago and oceans away. Epigenetics is an area of research that focuses on inherited changes to the genome that don't alter the underlying sequence. Environmental factors and traumatic experiences can turn genes on and off, and the modified genome can be passed on to daughter cells in future generations. This validates the folk saying that "it runs in the family," but it does not doom those of us with intergenerational trauma. Our choices matter. Remember, the work is for descendants we may never meet. When the Corporeal Soul returns to the soil and the Ethereal Soul goes to the invisible realms, we live on in our children's cells.

Like DNA in biomedicine, Jing is an inherited foundation for human life. Translated as "kidney essence," it functions as an ancestral template and a source of power. Profoundly connected to the spirit of Willpower Zhi and the marrow of our bones, Jing circulates in the eight extraordinary meridians of the body. This precious resource is one of the Three Treasures of vitality that facilitates hair growth, sexual function, longevity, and much more.

Chinese medical theory states that Jing is finite and cannot be replenished. For this reason, practices that conserve essence are important. Daoist esoteric practices, however, can potentially restore and augment Jing. Stories of eighty-year-old men growing new sets of teeth through cultivation of Jing give me hope. It is certainly not easy—ancestor work rarely is—but heritage is not destiny.

Both Daoism and biomedicine affirm the possibility of ancestral transformation. Through our choices, we can course-correct for ourselves and those who come after us. Seeking healing, we can awaken dormant potential within the genomes we carry. Through spiritual cultivation, we can preserve the distilled wisdom and strength of our ancestors.

By finding ways to consider what we have inherited from our ancestors— and how we can build a future that will benefit those who will inherit it— we can counteract the overreliance on individual agency that has caused so much trauma in our contemporary world. Ancestral perspective has the potential for collective healing. Many Indigenous peoples make major decisions in terms of impact on future descendants. For example, a well-established Haudenosaunee philosophy specifically considers seven generations from the present moment. By moving from a sense of responsibility to children yet to be born, ancestrally centered societies preserve life on earth. Those of us who are settlers can reckon with the past and choose a collective mindset to pass on to our descendants. As we expand beyond the myopic focus on individual gain, we turn our gaze toward infinity. Connected to those who have gone before us and those to come, we don't have to chase cravings to numb loneliness.

We are never alone.

ANCESTRAL RECONNECTION EXERCISE

1. What ancestors of good character do you know of? Take some time to ask relatives and/or do genealogical research.

2. What family practices and traditions connected your ancestors to the cycles of nature, to the land, to loved ones, and to the invisible realms?

3. What community roles or professions have your ancestors traditionally fulfilled?

4. Reflect on what you know of your lineages. What liberatory, high-integrity themes do you notice? Archetypes? Patterns?

ANCESTOR ALTAR

If compatible with your spiritual beliefs, I invite you to use the imagery and objects you find in your research to create a small ancestor altar. A simple, accessible practice I learned from my mother is to set a plate of food aside for the ancestors at every meal. If you don't know what to cook for them, Priestess-in-training Omiṣeye Williams says, "They like what you like." Even without a separate plate, you can feed them at the altar that you embody. By savoring your meal with them in mind, they receive the offering.

You may choose to gather images of adopted, biological, and chosen ancestors and place them on your ancestor altar. When it's time for you to face a challenge, encounter fear, or need strength, speak their names aloud.

Although they no longer inhabit physical forms, their names and images beckon their consciousness to you.

Your ancestor altar might include any of the following suggested elements, or none. This list is meant as a springboard if you feel stuck, not a definitive template.

- Art or photography depicting deceased relatives and chosen ancestors
- An altar cloth or traditional textiles
- A plant or vase of flowers
- Water, alcohol, or ancestors' preferred beverages
- Candles safely positioned where they won't start a fire
- A gong, bell, drum, rattle, or other instrument
- Sacred symbols of your cultural heritage
- A pot of soil or stones from land where your ancestors lived
- Food offerings (you can place these in a sealed food storage container if you can't risk attracting insects or animals)
- Ethically sourced fragrances such as Grandma's favorite perfume, incense, essential oils, copal, myrrh

Celestial Visualization

Draw your attention to the soles of your feet. With each exhale, release physical and emotional tension and let your muscles relax. Allow your body to soften, and notice how the earth carries the burdens you put down. Feel the crown of your head tingle as moonbeams caress your forehead, washing over and through you with cool, soothing light. Say your name three times, and you are in your sacred grove.

A fountain of lapis lazuli overflows with clear water, splashing diamonds that sparkle in the moonlight. You approach and cup some water in your hands, taking in your reflection rippling with stars above. At the crown of your head, a star begins to glow. Crystalline clear light begins to radiate across light-years to join with your upper elixir field. Celestial energy from the North Star asks permission to enter your energy body and, with your consent, permeates your being.

You feel limitless heavenly source Qi over-flowing through your pores, revitalizing you on a subatomic level. Your mitochondria dance with joy as all your organ systems are restored. You pop two corks in the soles of your feet, and waste Qi drains out, leaving you weightless. The water molecules of your being glow, your reflection showing you as a light being. Several feet around your body in all directions, pure light from the North Star cleanses and heals.

Take some time to invite this starlight to those parts of your body where you need extra support. Feel the North Star giving you everything you need and more. When you are ready, thank Polaris and feel its light recede just far enough that you can always call upon it as needed.

Shining from head to toe, you lift your eyes from the water's surface to the sky above. The seven stars of the Drinking Gourd glitter, pouring a soft rain of amethyst light that soothes every aspect of your being.

Refreshed to your core, you return to the central mandala and take three luxurious, deep breaths. Invoking your name three times, you return to your daily life.

PRENATAL ESSENCE

The Kidneys, the Yin Water organ, are said to be the root of Yin and Yang in the body. Prenatal Essence 精 is located in the Kidneys, an inheritance from one's parents. The ancestors give us our physical bodies and constitutions, the material conditions to live human lives. In the lives they lived, we find a wealth of knowledge. Their mistakes show us pitfalls to avoid. Their triumphs expand our fields of possibility. At the same time, we are more than the sum of all those who came before us. We are connected to them; we are of them; but we also have our own Heart Spirit 心神.

In this chapter, we will focus on what's working in your lineage. Suggested jumping-off points:

- Look up images of the lands to which your ancestors are indigenous. Save, clip from magazines, and/or print those that you find especially beautiful.

- Seek out elders and ask their permission to record stories and confirm genealogy. Use your creativity to represent your family tree.

DREAMWORK

The Water element relates to the depths of the collective unconscious, so this is an appropriate place to discuss dreamwork. The Heart Spirit 心神 rests in the Blood while we sleep, dancing with our Ethereal Soul 魂. This psychic interplay of the conscious mind with the subtle intuitive sense can reveal profound insights. If you don't remember your dreams, don't worry. From a Chinese medical perspective, this can indicate that your Heart Spirit is well rooted. By softening your gaze and waiting to start using your brain to plan your day, memories of your dreams might show themselves more easily.

I experience dream memories like shy creatures that wait to emerge until I make space for them.

If possible, ease your entrance and exit from dreaming realms with a gentle immersion as opposed to a cannonball into sleep. Dimming the lights and reducing the use of technology before bed assists with sleep hygiene, though not everyone has the privilege of time for an extended bedtime ritual. Simply asking benevolent ancestors for guidance before sleeping can bring illuminating revelations.

Keeping a dream journal helps track patterns and archetypes as they surface. Try drawing with your nondominant hand, collaging the locations and beings that appear, and writing freely. Rather than relying on dream dictionaries based on dominant social symbolism, I suggest creating your own dictionary based on the cultural meanings of your ancestry. Keep a playful curiosity throughout the day, staying open to symbols from your dreams.

Ancestral communication through dreams can be like speaking across a language barrier. The imagery and stories ancestors use to express themselves might not make linear sense initially. Try following strands of meaning through free association in your journal. Of course, not everything is a message. Watch out for the Water emotion of fear and the human tendency to focus on the worst-case scenario. Sometimes the brain is just processing experiences from your day. Observing your dream life will help you discern the psychic from the mundane.

If your dreamworld is an unsafe place, there are remedies. Softly massaging the area behind and under the ear activates Peaceful Sleep 安眠, a point indicated for sleep issues and emotional disturbance. A point called Strict Exchange 厲兌 on the second toe calms the spirit for dreaming. It is located on the lateral, dorsal aspect of the toe, which means the point is on the top of the foot, closer to the little toe than the big toe. You can apply pressure just near the bottom corner of the toenail, closer to the little toe. You may use your right hand to draw three horizontal lines ☰, the symbol for Heaven 乾 Qian, above your pillow for protection. Facing the west, you can envision a majestic white tiger descending a staircase of light from Venus and then touching its head to your chest. From your lungs, a metallic white light expands to form a shimmering mesh that guards against harm while allowing in what you need.

When you lie down to sleep, you may place your hands above the lower and middle elixir fields for protection. The lower energy center is slightly below the navel, and the middle is around the sternum. Lying on your right side allows gravity to draw Blood into your Liver, which can help with dream-disturbed sleep. Qigong instructor Edward Sullivan suggests envisioning the seven stars of the Drinking Gourd constellation pouring amethyst light upon you, cleansing all that you do not need.

If you wake up from a nightmare or consistently encounter terrors in your sleep, you may apply pressure or pinch below your nose in the frenulum area, the area between your nose and upper lip. This is Humanity's Center 人中, a "ghost point" according to famous physician Sun Si-Miao. Ancient acupuncturists regarded this as one of the most useful acupressure points, and it is the principal point for restoring Yin and Yang to harmony as well as reviving consciousness. It's a good idea to repeat this in multiples of three, such as 9, 21, or 36.

WATER HEALING

Issues with the Water element often relate to reproductive health, aging, hearing, hair growth, and bone problems. You might want to refer to the resources in this section if you or your loved ones manifest cardinal symptoms of the Water element: urinary difficulty, hair loss, premature hair graying, impotence, osteoporosis, memory challenges, hearing loss, or debilitating fear. As you may notice, these conditions often appear in elders, who are in the winter season of their lives. Daoist and Chinese medical texts contain an abundance of strategies for longevity and vitality into old age, so winter is not to be feared.

More than half of the human body is water, so water healing can begin right where you are. Your intra- and extracellular fluid is the embodiment of ☵ 坎 Kan, the trigram of Water. By gently stroking circles around your lower and mid-back, you can awaken Kidney Qi. Feeling for the bottom of your rib cage, you can locate the kidneys and the adrenals, which sit atop them. A simple back massage stimulates the Urinary Bladder channel, opening the Greater Yang 太陽 meridian. A trusted partner can apply gentle, constant, moving pressure on the vertical line midway between the scapula and the spine. When you are giving this massage, begin with minimal pressure, deepen into the level of pressure that the recipient desires, and gradually reduce the pressure before lifting your hands away. This will awaken the Back Shu points, which are portals to organs and meridians that flow throughout the body. By applying acupressure here, you are practicing Chinese massage 推拿 Tuīná, which has supported human health for at least three thousand years. This simple exercise is called 按 àn, a linear moving manipulation.

The Kidney and Urinary Bladder meridians exchange Yin and Yang Qi on the feet, so foot massage can be another supportive practice. Soaking your feet in an Epsom salt bath benefits the Kidney and other Yin organs, especially during winter. Placing your fingers on the dorsal aspect (top) of the foot, you can use your thumbs on the soles of the feet to press outward from the centerline. Try giving extra attention to the area just below the ball of the foot, where Gushing Spring 湧泉 lies. This is the first point on the Kidney channel, a place where we receive Qi from the earth and release waste Qi for the earth to compost. You can breathe in and out through this point to allow waste Qi to drain out of the body and receive support from the earth. You may visualize popping a cork in this region and all your fatigue, anger, and so on being sucked out into a fertile compost pile below. Imagining that you are squeezing toothpaste out of a tube, alternate your thumbs from the sole across the ball of the foot toward each toe. When you reach the tip of each toe, use the proximal knuckles (the joints closest to the palm) of your index and middle finger to gently squeeze and pull away from the foot. It may make a snapping sound, which is normal.

Near the little toe on the lateral side of the foot, you'll find Foot Connecting Valley 足通谷 in the depression in front of and below the fifth metatarsal-phalangeal joint. This is the bone that you feel at the base of your little toe where it meets the top of your foot. The Water point on the Urinary Bladder channel, this is a "horary point" with particular influence over the meridians and organs of the Water element. It will be especially effective between three and seven p.m., the hours when Qi is moving through the Water meridians. A Ying-Spring point, Foot Connecting Valley 足通谷 is a place where Qi glides. If you feel chaotic, frightened, or manic, with excess Yang Qi in your head, this point can bring balance.

Sound healing for the Water element is ideal during the hours of three to seven p.m. and in the winter. Different sources describe the healing sound of the Water element as *Fff* or *Chuan*. You can try both and discover which you prefer, depending on the day. Inhaling deep into your lower back, exhale with your teeth lightly positioning to make the consonant sound of *Fff*. The air leaving your lungs filters through your teeth and benefits your Water meridian and organs. After a thorough inhale, begin with the *ch* sound and allow your entire exhale to unfurl on the *uan* sound.

Culinary remedies for the Water element are largely salty and best in wintertime. According to the Yo San University clinic, stews and soups, yams, braised meat, and rice protect internal warmth. Longan fruit, sticky rice, red dates, and walnuts are traditional aids for cold. Adding leeks, ginger, and scallions can scatter chills. Ginseng powerfully tonifies Source Qi and calms the Heart Spirit. Walnuts 胡桃仁 are beneficial for sensations of cold with back and knee pain, urinary frequency, constipation in the elderly or following a febrile disorder, cough or wheezing, and constipation. It's not a good idea to eat walnuts with strong tea if you're experiencing loose stool or if you feel any heat. Adzuki beans 赤小豆 are a food herb that can reduce edema and address urinary difficulty so that Water flows correctly in the body. Rose hips 金櫻子 benefit Kidney Essence and are a wonderful tea (make sure to eat some longan fruit with them, because rose hips are not tonifying).

THE GATES OF LIFE

In Chinese medicine, the Kidneys are connected to the Gate of Life 命門 Ming Men. Located between the Kidneys or the right Kidney, depending on which classical text you study, Ming Men fire is essential for the harmonious functioning of the body. Associated with Kidney Yang, this vital force energizes the lower core of the body as it performs essential functions of digestion and release of waste.

This sacred flame is also important for sexual health. In Daoism, sexuality is not shameful or unclean. There is a long, documented history of "dual cultivation" practices by which Daoists harmonized Yin and Yang through intimacy. The Gate of Life and our erotic power are integral aspects of human existence. Sexual expression can heal, and it made possible every generation that led to you.

This book provides only general guidance for working with the Gate of Life, because physical intimacy is potent. You can find information on Daoist sexual alchemy elsewhere. I suggest engaging those tools with great care, because they have been refined over thousands of years. It's also important to do due diligence, checking the accuracy of source texts and qualifications of teachers.

Harnessing the vibrant potential of the Gate of Life can be simple. The act of kissing connects individuals' respective Sea of Yang and Sea of Yin, extraordinary meridians that are the first to form after conception and relate to our "pre-heaven essence." Jeffrey C. Yuen teaches that the extraordinary vessels relate to destiny, as the "first ancestry" within the meridian system. The Governing Vessel and the Conception Vessel form a microcosmic orbit in the body when they meet within the mouth. This is why meditators place their tongue on the soft palate, to circulate Yin and Yang freely. The first points on the channels of the Sea of Yang and the Sea of Yin are located close to the anus and reproductive organs, where sexual partners often stimulate each other in unconscious acupressure. The Conception Vessel runs along the front of the body, and the Governing Vessel runs up the back, so different sexual positions activate these foundational meridians.

In physical intimacy, partners open the lower gates near the sexual organs and the upper gates of the mouth. Nipple play and emotional intimacy also activate the area of the middle energy center near the heart. This engages the three elixir fields and transfers important substances. Saliva, semen, and other fluids exchanged in play have energetic properties. After Qi cultivation, Daoists swallow their saliva because the water is believed to transform into a jade or golden elixir. Acupuncture professors jokingly recommend eating steak after ejaculation because semen is closely related to Kidney Essence, a precious substance within Chinese medical theory.

I invite you to incorporate this information into reverence for yourself and any sexual partners as living microcosms of celestial energy, covered with constellations and energy rivers.

Just by bringing awareness to the act of play, you can use intention to transform your activity into a healing session. Enjoy and be prudent. A Chinese folk saying goes: "The water that carries a boat is the same that drowns it."

CHAPTER 11

THE DIVE

In Chinese medicine, Water and Metal make respiration possible. The Lungs are meant to inhale deeply enough that the Kidneys anchor the Qi. Breathing into the lower abdomen energizes the region of the body that corresponds to the Water element. This reservoir of calm is a counterpoint to rapid breathing centered in the chest, which acupuncturists sometimes diagnose as "Kidney failing to grasp Qi." Using your diaphragm, visualize your inhale reaching calm ocean waves in your lower abdomen. This is parasympathetic breathing, which soothes the autonomic nervous system when in a fight-or-flight reaction. Intentional deep breathing is associated with reduced symptoms of anxiety and greater relaxation.

Like all the energetic phases, Water functions best when nourished by its generating element and balanced by its controlling element. Metal generates Water as the Lungs bring fresh Qi to the Kidneys. When in excess, the Earth element contains the riptide as riverbanks hold the river. Should a flash flood of terror send cortisol coursing through your bloodstream, try to bring your awareness to gravity. Feel your connection to the ground, and draw your inhale into the lower abdomen. Root in the material reality of your circumstances, noticing tangible anchors around your body with your physical senses. Earth element's spirit, the Intellect, is an ally whose practicality can alleviate fear. Tending to Metal and Earth can restore Water to harmonious flow, and tidal waves of terror will dissipate gently.

ON FEAR AND COURAGE

The Water element is profoundly ancestral and corresponds to fear. Our inherited "prenatal essence" originates in the Kidneys, where it gives life to Source Qi. This primordial energy travels throughout the body and plays a role in vital functions. Switching from a Chinese medical lens to a psychological perspective, deeply rooted familial patterns repeat across generations and impact all areas of our lives. Survival of the family line is an imperative that drives people to overcome incredible odds with the determination of the Willpower 志. The ancient will to carry on is a powerful resource best used consciously. Survival instincts based on fear have kept previous generations alive but might not necessarily serve the present moment. When out of alignment, these old anxieties are still deserving of respect. The Water element fear of losing what is precious may have prevented reckless Fire element risk-taking from getting out of hand. Breathwork can help calm frightened ancestral energy.

In ancestor work, spiritual bypassing prevents real healing. Intergenerational trauma does not get better when ignored. That's how suffering continues for centuries. Facing the legacies of ancestors who committed harm can bring up shame, guilt, and other difficult emotions. This chapter is designed to support you in dealing with these kinds of challenges bit by bit, through grief into action. James Baldwin wrote, "Not everything that is faced can be changed, but nothing can be changed until it is faced." The most meaningful healing happens in reality when we reckon with what is. Transformation is possible. The Five Elements are phases of change, and together we follow their cycle toward greater alignment with the best of your lineage.

It will take courage. Honesty with yourself is essential, and no one can force that. The rewards of your bravery are commensurate to the commitment you put into your healing. It is possible for you to be fully integrated with your ancestral legacy, empowered by both your ancestors' mistakes and their triumphs.

Breath Visualization

Place your palms on your lower belly and imagine crystalline blue water filling the space below your belly button. Rich with life, this ocean shimmers below azure skies. Reflected in the gentle waves, a white cloud brings shade and balances the brightness of the sun. This cloud glows silver in your chest, illuminating your lungs with radiance. Breathing in, feel your palms easily expand outward as a soft rain falls from your chest to your lower abdomen. Breathing out, sparkling droplets evaporate from the water's surface to join the cloud. Feel this sweet, natural reciprocity within you, and stay with this visualization for at least nine breaths.

Just as you and I and all the matter in the universe share a common origin, so do all our ancestors. All the beings since the first single-celled organism on this planet are kindred. Everything we know and are is stardust that has been rearranged in countless forms for incomprehensible scales of time.

In this chapter, you will be revisiting the themes of integrity you have discovered in your life and your lineage. And if your ancestral line has moved away from the undifferentiated Source 無極, there is a way back. When we get lost, we retrace our steps. There is a road home.

INHERITANCE EXERCISE

1. What are the positive patterns in your family line? Who are your people when you are at your best?

2. What legacies of integrity and honor do you want to carry on?

3. Who can support you in continuing honorable legacies?

4. What are specific, consistent actions you can take to continue positive ancestral patterns?

5. How will you reward yourself for taking action to carry forward the integrity of your lineage?

CHALLENGES IN ANCESTOR WORK

Ancestor work nowadays is rarely simple. As we uncover the wounds of generations of aggression between groups of people, you may find that your ancestral line has perpetrated injustices, or that you are part of a group that has inherited generations upon generations of trauma. This is an opportunity to reach back and find a language based in the origins of your ancestral line, perhaps before colonialism, chattel slavery, or genocide pushed your ancestors away from their unique traditions, rituals, and spirituality. For example, people whose ancestors survived bondage can use spiritual methods to bridge the void and connect generations. Hoodoo, Vodun, Ifá, and other Afro-diasporic religions have the medicine to divine across space-time. Jewish mysticism, Tibetan Buddhism, and European folk herbalism are just a few other examples of rich traditions your ancestors may have practiced. Daoism has been my entry point to my spiritual inheritance, and I hope this book might be a bridge to your own ancient medicine.

If you don't know of a reliable spiritual practitioner with the relevant expertise, there are other ways to come into conscious contact. Baba Falokun Faṣẹgun, priest of Ifá, says that when colonizers destroyed shrines and took people away from their homelands, the body became the altar. The place we face when we pray can be the mirror where countless generations express themselves through our physical traits. Your own body as a living descendant is holy ground for ancestors whose memory lives in the strands of your cells. They may appear in dreams or synchronicities to reveal who they are. Pay attention and note ancestral messages in your journal.

ADOPTED ANCESTRY

Can people who aren't adoptees have adopted ancestors? Yes, but it's best to get this confirmed by a trustworthy, well-trained spiritual practitioner with an analysis of power. It's easy to believe our own wishful thinking, and claiming adopted ancestors can be a tactic to justify cultural appropriation. If upheld by a diviner of integrity, ideally themselves a descendant of the adopting ancestors, spiritual adoption comes with a responsibility to show up for the living descendants. To honor the adopting lineage, practice solidarity with people who embody the cellular memory of the dead. I suggest not speaking publicly about "spiritual adoption," as it can be very painful for those whose bodies experience violence for being living descendants.

Family dysfunction is another widespread obstacle to ancestral healing. When relatives hurt you and your loved ones, it can be excruciating because there is no ultimate escape. While we live in these bodies, we cannot change our DNA or divorce our families. It is essential to admit the reality of abuse and the necessity of going no-contact when relatives are dangerous. Since harmful power dynamics in the present may spring from past generations, many people struggle with ancestor work. Lineage can feel like a cage.

If this is the case for you, I support you in taking the space you need. Reaching out to relatives living or dead should happen on survivors' terms and timeline. If the family member who knows the genealogy is unsafe, perhaps a supportive relative can ask them for the information. When there is nobody who can be trusted in one's family of origin, then spiritual strategies can apply. Priestess Iya Fayomi Oṣundoyin Egbeyemi says that no lineage begins with trauma. There may not be baptism records, photos, or old stories from that time, but we all have ancestors who lived with integrity and mutual care. Through cultivation and ritual, you can connect to those spirits and open a channel for ancestral support without sacrificing your boundaries. If necessary, leapfrog over the known generations and call upon ancient forebears. You may be the first descendant to call upon them in a while, and they may be sleeping deeply, but they may become your greatest cheerleaders as you build relationships across the space-time continuum.

Use the exercise below to reflect on your lineage—the negative and positive aspects of what you see when you reach toward your ancestral line. If you discover that your ancestors have done things that have been harmful to others, now is the time to acknowledge that fact and work to change future chapters of your ancestral story.

ANCESTRAL REFLECTION EXERCISE

1. Did your family begin to stray from your connection to Earth-centered practices? What was happening in that era?

2. How has your lineage missed the mark in your relationship to land, ecosystems, and more-than-human beings?

3. How has your lineage missed the mark in committed partnerships?

4. How has your lineage missed the mark in parenting?

5. How has your lineage missed the mark in how you treat elders and disabled people?

6. How has your lineage missed the mark in your participation in society?

Remember that human beings are and have always been complex. In the legacies of those gone before, there are very likely both survivors and perpetrators—often both in the same person. Holding the paradox may stretch the heart until it feels like breaking. There is no way to separate and cast out the harm doers who were part of our lineage from those we politically approve of. All of what went before is always present. And it can be transformed.

There must never be any apologism for ancestral harm. At the same time, we can identify the person's actions as unforgivable without deciding that their souls are beyond mercy. Actions of harm can be shifted by making amends, and so long as we are alive, we can be the ones who take the actions that redress the harm. This is the focus of the element Wood.

BEST PRACTICES

This section is a distillation of my twelve years of spiritual seeking across continents and modalities. As you dive into ancestor work, I hope that these suggestions might be a map to avoid cliffs and find oases. However, my personal experience and studies cannot encompass all that you may encounter. I offer them as tips from a friend, and fully support you in following your own road.

First, I suggest focusing on lineage healing and alignment with your individual path 道. By beginning with the legacies and healing potential in our own bodies, we can catalyze transformation for our communities. This foundation reduces the risk of rituals backfiring due to spiritual impatience. It also grounds us with the discernment to identify scammers masquerading as shamans. From a place of simultaneous empowerment and humility, we can then consider what esoteric traditions or practices might support our growth. Ancestor work roots us in the reality that we are in human form and spiritual healing happens from within our bodies. Our ancestors gave us life, and the Heart Spirit 心神 reigns from within our chest cavity. Courageous engagement with challenging aspects of your ancestry, past, and personality can transform your body into a sanctuary.

It's important to note that embodied practice isn't accessible to everyone, however. Dissociation from physical reality is a necessary coping mechanism in cases of unbearable trauma, so survivors may not have access to safety and resources to "be in the body."

If that is the case for you, please honor the pace and direction of your healing journey. Rather than excavating old traumas, getting to safety is of course the priority. Building a support system, asking for help, and speaking your truth are spiritual acts. Reclaiming your body through mirror work and pleasure practices might be empowering if it feels right. By externalizing pain through art, exercise, ritual, or activism, you can reduce the transmission of unprocessed trauma to future generations. You also might ask benevolent ancestors to show you how to alchemize your pain into medicine, reclaiming your story and reshaping the world. Sometimes, our individual suffering is connected to larger issues that we can join with others to address.

Although focusing on human challenges might seem less exciting than invoking awe-inspiring deities, it can prevent serious problems. The metaphysical world is real; indigenous cultures worldwide have always known this. In many indigenous cultures, intuitives are prepared and identified in order to serve the community by connecting with the spiritual world via techniques and rituals refined over time. Without these systems in place, mayhem can ensue.

Making up rituals based on information cobbled from the internet is understandable, but it can have severe consequences. For this reason, I do not advise using blood, trying to open portals, or invoking energies without supervision and guidance from a trustworthy teacher who is grounded in an existing tradition. Ancient divinities are not Santa Claus or imaginary friends, but actual energies who manifest when summoned, whether or not you're ready.

Wonderful healing can result from keeping it simple and seeking an established lineage. Devoting time to study with trustworthy elders in a specific tradition is an act of respect for indigenous ways of learning and doing. Innovation without a grounding in the past is unmoored.

Centering in your own lineage healing can also protect against spiritual scams. Predators and the selfish view the trauma of spiritual disinheritance as a market to exploit. Messages from strangers along the lines of "I have a message from your ancestors" are a red flag. You, yourself, are the first point of contact with your ancestors; their legacy is alive in every cell of your body. Someone you've never met claiming to be a go-between is often unscrupulous. There are valid ancestral connection rituals and honorable diviners, and it is worth waiting until you find them. As the vessel of your bloodlines, you don't need to give your power away to others.

Connection with your ancestors is your inheritance and can be similar to relationship-building with the living. Clarifying your understanding of ancestral messages takes time and is worth practice. Regular consultation of the I Ching or a culturally appropriate divination method of your own ancestry will help you hone your awareness. Notice how synchronicity and guidance appear, and experience will hone your awareness of the ever-present metaphysical in the everyday.

Differentiating between one's own neuroses, messages solely from your own ancestors for you, and messages for someone else is challenging. It is far too easy to delude ourselves into believing we are receiving downloads for others, and there are spiritual energies that take advantage of the particularly dangerous combination of naïveté and arrogance.

Simplicity and practicality can work miracles. Sweeping the floor with intentionality is a ritual. Integrity brings more good fortune than buying expensive ingredients to perform a multistep ceremony. Honesty with oneself and others, interrupting intergenerational patterns of harm, and doing what you can to seed justice is sacred.

Starting with human challenges and problems clears metaphysical space for blessings. Before consulting a psychic, oracle cards, or the I Ching, try sitting quietly and looking inside yourself. Ask the ancient wisdom within you, or whatever you believe in, to be guided toward your purpose and teachers. You can request to recognize spiritual teachers and lessons, and to be ready when they show up.

CHAPTER 12

THE RELEASE

As a living lineage bearer, you are the steward of your genetic inheritance. You have responsibility to and bonds with your ancestors, as well as your own agency. You are not bound to continue the trajectories of past generations. Their time has passed. They granted you the materials for a life, including the gift of their errors, which are guideposts. For as long as you have breath in your lungs, you have the capacity to choose what you do with that inheritance.

Every cell of your body can be a site of ancestor work. The choices you make each day activate or suppress possibilities in your DNA, epigenetically altering your genome. Inheritance is not destiny. Whether or not you pass on your DNA to future generations, your ancestors' genetic material is with you right now. So many bloodlines have died out, but they and you are here at this moment.

RENEWAL

At all scales of existence, water renews life on this planet. Throughout your day, you can transform simple interactions with water into reverential ones. Before drinking, take a breath to express gratitude and lift up a prayer for all beings to have access to clean drinking water. You may request that the water remove from your body both physical and energetic toxins, the Kidney and Urinary Bladder clearing what you no longer need. Bathing with intention not only clears off the dirt but can cleanse spiritually.

INTERGENERATIONAL NARRATIVE TRANSFORMATION EXERCISE

1. Water changes form: it can be gas, liquid, or solid. How have you changed form throughout your lifetime? How has your lineage changed form? How would you like to proceed, individually and collectively, knowing that you don't have to repeat old patterns?

2. Write the saga of your lineage thus far. Reflect on all that you have learned. Leave nothing out. Zoom out across the space-time continuum to perceive the macrocosm. What was happening regionally and globally as your ancestors adapted to the changes of their time?

3. What beliefs, stories, patterns, and behaviors does your lineage need to release? Write, draw, record yourself speaking, sculpt, embody; externalize in whatever modality feels best to you.

Serenity Visualization

Settle into a comfortable position and let your eyelids drop. Your attention gravitates to the nourishing, steady support of the earth below you. With each exhale, you release more weight to the welcoming earth. From above, moonbeams kiss your forehead and bathe you inside and out. After three repetitions of your name, you find yourself in your sacred grove.

Gazing around, you notice a clear pool of crystalline water. Indigo and lapis lazuli depths reflect dazzling stars. You notice the stars glimmering in droplets that begin to rise from the surface in spirals. Evaporating upward, beads of water resemble necklaces weaving together as strands of DNA. They condense into a royal blue cloud, and a regal tortoise emerges. This is the Mysterious Warrior 北方玄武 Běifāng Xuánwǔ, guardian of the north. Its ancient eyes communicate primordial wisdom and calm strength. The patterns on its shell are whorls of ocean waves. When you place your hand on the shell, deep blue light fills your lower back, abdomen, and reproductive area. Pain evaporates and profound serenity takes its place. A gentle rain begins to fall, cleansing you of intergenerational suffering. As the drizzle stops, you see a twinkle on the northern horizon from Mercury, the "water star." It reminds you that your being is liquid starlight. Azure starlight from Mercury anoints your head and pours in a waterfall down your back. From below your feet, sapphire light rises to trace the inner aspect of your leg. It then ascends the center of your abdomen to your collarbone, renewing the Water meridians of your body.

You thank the Mysterious Warrior and return to the central mandala of your grove. After taking several deep breaths, you say your name three times and find yourself renewed as you move on with your day.

The block universe theory supposes that all times are co-present. So, following this line of thought, we can imagine that although your ancient ancestors are not alive at this moment, their existence is simply at another point on the space-time continuum. Within you, they live on in the heart of every cell. When we love ourselves unconditionally, we are also expressing love for the pantheon of ancestors in our embodied memory. (Unconditional love is not an endorsement or enabling of abusive behavior, but an energy of radical care in recognition of beings' inviolable, inherent worth.)

At some point before or during your current lifetime, your ancestors have probably gone through trauma and loss. Some say that pain travels through families until someone is ready—and has the emotional regulation tools and conditions—to feel it. In Chinese medicine, some of the ancient scholars say that unwept tears stay in the body and become illness. Experiences of overwhelming intensity, if not processed and released, can (in a metaphysical, Chinese medicine sense) enter the deepest meridians and the Kidney Essence 精 that parents pass onto their children. If you ever find yourself weeping harder than the circumstances seem to warrant, or carrying tenderness that seems to have no source you can remember, it may be something that previous generations were unable to release.

I suggest setting specific, manageable increments of time to feel these feelings and let them leave your energetic-somatic system. Whether in talk therapy, at an energy healing session, or with someone you trust who agrees to hold space for you, create a deliberate container to siphon out the emotions bit by bit. It can be overwhelming to try to do it all at once—that's probably why previous generations couldn't process it! But as we gently, consistently drain out the trauma, the sense of pent-up pressure eases. Setting a timer to cry or shake in front of your altar can help. Little by little, we begin to feel lighter, less weighed down and stuck.

There's no need to try to intellectually understand or pinpoint the cause of every emotion. By definition, feelings aren't rational, and they are still valid. Usually, they just need to be witnessed, acknowledged, and comforted. If possible, I suggest reaching out to a trustworthy person (not related to you) who has some space from the intensity and can hold a container for this very important work.

If you know details about the events and causes of wounding previous generations experienced, it can be healing to give yourself the medicine they needed. My ancestors survived the Irish potato famine, and I entered an outpatient eating disorder treatment program decades later because I wasn't eating enough. Each time I nourish myself with delicious, abundant food, I am providing the ancestors in my DNA with the nutrition they needed. As cycle-breakers, it is important for us to interrupt patterns by introducing new and different experiences so that we pass on the sense memory of being well, held, whole, and supported. Whatever rituals of healing you identify, call upon your accountability team to help you consistently give yourself the medicine your lineage needs. Repetition, rather than one intense and dramatic experience, may be necessary for the body to believe that it is safe and provided for.

Epigenetic Release Ritual

By now, you may have an ancestor altar. If not, please go to a place you feel safe and adapt the following ritual in accordance with your own beliefs. This is a suggested practice; it is more important that you attune with your own inner compass than follow an external procedure. Your own body is an ancestral altar at the crossroads of generations.

1. *Find a time and space that feels intimate and where you won't be disturbed. If it is aligned, invite your chosen family.*

2. *Fill a glass or bowl with clean ice and bring it with you to your ritual space.*

3. *Take at least three deep breaths, inhaling deep blue healing light from Mercury into your lower back, the location of the Water organs.*

4. *Name the chosen and biological ancestors with whom you feel warmth, support, understanding, and kinship.*

5. *Call upon ancestors whose names you don't know, but who love you and want to help you. This includes*

myriad spirits over hundreds of thousands of years. Notice if you feel them awakening and answering your call.

6.   Ask whatever you believe in (I suggest the North Star if you're not sure) to guide those ancestors in need of healing back home to their highest integrity.

7.   Feel into your heart space until you feel your intent is at its clearest. Explain to your body and your ancestors that you are here for lineage healing through transformation and release.

8.   Read aloud the story of your lineage.

9.   Thank all your ancestors for giving you a body and a life. Express gratitude for what you genuinely appreciate about your inheritance.

10.   Read what your lineage needs to release into the ice.

11.   Put the ice in a pot to boil and speak to Fire and Water about what you love. We are using Fire to transform the element Water using Fire's energy of love. Explain to your ancestors that you are coming from love. You may add herbs if you know plant allies that support in healing, but there is no need to do so.

12. *When the water is boiling, carefully remove it from the fire and let the steam rise in front of your ancestor altar, in your sanctuary space, or outside. (Caution: don't leave boiling water outside unless you are there to supervise.)*

13. *Notice that the water has changed form from solid to liquid to gas. Reflect on how your ancestors were once matter and are now ephemeral, and on your capacity to be an agent of change while incarnate in a material body.*

14. *Inhale deep blue light into your lower back, consciously exhaling what you and your ancestors are releasing.*

15. *When the water has cooled, you may use it to water plants, moving the energy through the generating cycle from Water to Wood.*

Part Five

WOOD

Love in Action

Initiates new beginnings

Expands and breaks through obstacles

Rises ever toward the sun

Planet: Jupiter 木星 Mù Xīng

Direction: East

Season: Spring

Guardian: Azure Dragon 東方青龍 Dōng Fāng Qing Lóng

Lunar mansions: Horn 角 Jiǎo, Neck 亢 Kàng, Root 氐 Dǐ, Room 房 Fáng, Heart 心 Xīn, Tail 尾 Wěi, Winnowing Basket 箕 Jī

Color: Green

Emotion: Anger

Organs: Liver, Gallbladder

Spirit: Ethereal Soul 魂 Hun

Trigrams ☴ Wind/Wood 巽 Xun, ☳ Thunder 震 Zhen

Affirmation: I am honorable and purposeful.

CHAPTER 13

BLOOD HEALING

As you move through the chapters in the element Wood, consider moving your body before or after you complete the exercises. The element Wood loves to grow in all directions, and physical movement allows stagnant Qi to flow everywhere it needs to go.

To connect with the element Wood, face the east. With intent, you can reach out to Jupiter for green energy and invite it into the space under your right breast, where the Liver and Gallbladder reside. The shade of green that appears in your mind's eye is that which best supports you. Some days you might receive rich emerald light, and others the delicate jade of new leaves. Allow this energy to support your Liver-Gallbladder system in detoxifying your being physically, emotionally, and spiritually. The light may roam freely within your mind's eye, because this is the quality of Wood. It moves in all directions as trees spread roots and twigs in 360 degrees from a central trunk. As the Wood Qi expands in spiraling tendrils, envision the radiating branches of your central nervous system sparkling in synaptic activity. As seedlings push through heavy sediment, let Jupiter's Qi unblock stagnant channels so that your vitality easily blossoms. The omnidirectional expansion roots you in the nourishing soil below while lifting you toward the warm embrace of sunlight above. Freshness and possibility surge through and beyond your form, a springtime spirit that you can access all year long.

Your Ethereal Soul shares this quality of dancing motion. The character for the Ethereal Soul swirls, a combination of the radicals for ghost and cloud. Described as "what comes and goes" 時起時落, this spirit's source is the paternal ancestry and joins the body three days after an infant is born. When a person dies, their Ethereal Soul lives on in the ancestral plane. The Ethereal Soul takes our inchoate desires from deep within and delivers them into plans for tangible projects. It flows through the psychic realms in dreamtime and animates our creative expression. When we extend beyond the individual ego in relationship to others, it is the Ethereal Soul that reaches out. Intuition and inspiration spring from the Ethereal Soul's psychic flow. As you move through this section, I invite you to give yourself permission to be fluid and spontaneous. Try drawing with your nondominant hand and notice what appears.

Wood energy is forceful and driven, cracking concrete and pushing up toward the celestial realms. The resilience and dynamism of Wood is a powerful resource for social change. As plants root deep into the soil before reaching for the heavens, you will draw strength from the good you discovered in your own bones. The lessons you have learned about familial and personal patterns will guide where your branches grow. From these boughs you may offer fruit and flowers—through works of art, children, or simply a life lived fully. With the power of saplings surging through packed soil, you will identify the people and groups that can support you in your life's work. Strengthened by these relationships, you will assess your skills to determine where you can be of greatest service. With the Wood element's vigor, you will prepare for obstacles and commit to continuous growth, choosing to channel your energy for greatest efficiency and sustainability.

The emotion of Wood is anger, which propels us to defend what is sacred to us. Societal condemnation of justified anger simply demonstrates its potency. What is powerful must be used with care, so practice relating to your anger with respect as well as restraint. As you proceed in your healing, I invite you to honor anger with attention and active listening. This power source can topple oppressive structures when wielded mindfully instead of indiscriminately. Audre Lorde distinguished anger from hatred by intent. Hatred seeks death. If anger springs from a love of life, it has messages and fuel for radical change. Stay attentive to the difference.

Your ancestors' time has passed. You have the sacred opportunity and responsibility to make choices in service of generations to come. What seeds will you plant? Sow melon, reap melon; sow beans, reap beans. 種瓜得瓜, 種豆得豆.

EMBODIED PRACTICES

The Wood element is medicine in motion. In the Wood season of spring, the Yellow Emperor's Inner Classic 黃帝內經 recommends awakening at daybreak. Power walks can align our bodies with the Yang, an active principle that is rising in the springtime. At whatever level is doable for you, explore physical movement. Walking is a form of taijiquan, even if you don't formally study Yang, Chen, or any other style of Chinese movement. The bilateral action of right and left feet integrates the Yin and Yang of the body. Exercising in nature will support your Wood Qi, and it can be as simple as doing gentle squats while facing a tree and/or the east. Water with a squeeze of lemon rejuvenates the Wood element after exertion.

In Chinese medicine, the Yin organ of the Wood element is strongly associated with Blood. Classical texts say that the Liver stores Blood, and Blood is the mother of Qi. In layperson's terms, this means that taking care of our Wood element is essential for vitality. As Wood Qi needs to flow freely, so does blood through our cardiovascular system. Cardiovascular exercise revitalizes our bodies as springtime brings life after winter. Vigorous exertion transports oxygen throughout the bloodstream and stimulates the production of endorphins, neurotransmitters that support well-being and can mitigate sensations of pain. I hope that you find ways to enjoy exercise for its gifts of vitality and happiness, without the pressure of modifying your shape to fit social norms.

Flourishing Visualization

Bring awareness to the earth holding you just tightly enough that you don't float away, and loosely enough that you are free. Notice any muscle tension and allow the earth to relieve you of your burdens. You feel a cord of light drawing your spine upward, opening spaciousness between your vertebrae. Shimmering moonlight pours from above, cleansing and nourishing you completely. Close your eyes.

Take three deep breaths, allowing yourself to make sound on your exhale. When you speak your name three times, you notice you are in your sacred grove.

Verdant foliage is blooming all around you. Plants are bejeweled with flowers and fruit, and tree roots form a comfortable seat. Leaning back against the trunk of a majestic tree, you feel the springy softness of moss as a pillow around your body. The canopy above sways with gentle breezes that tickle your cheek as sunbeams dapple the forest floor. Butterflies dance on playful gusts of wind as patterns of shade softly shift.

The firm roots below you embody the nourishing support of Earth, while sunlight distilled through layers of leaves replenishes your Yang Qi. From the east, you catch a glimpse of shining azure. Looking closer, you observe a majestic dragon with scales shimmering, eyes bright. Myriad shades of blue and green dazzle you as the dragon approaches with sinuous grace. With each step, flowers unfurl and fruit ripens on the vine. When this dragon stands before you, all you feel is openness and delight. The dragon's inclined head invites you to climb upon its back, and together you rise above the tree line, branches easily bending out of the way of your ascent. Rivers shimmer below as you witness the emerald canopy ripple in the wind. Buoyed by columns of air, you feel limitless and free.

When you are ready, you gently stroke the dragon's side, and it returns you to your sacred grove. It gently touches your lower right abdomen with a cerulean claw, and you notice your Liver glow with a glorious green light. Bowing goodbye, it spirals upward, following a jade bridge to Jupiter.

In the central mandala of your grove, repeat your name three times. Shift gently in your seat and slowly flutter your eyes open as you come back to the present moment.

Wood Element Kitchen Herbalism

Specific remedies will depend on individual constitution and health conditions, but there are some general principles. Here are a selection of excellent foods for blood healing in the Wood element:

Longan 龍眼肉: This is a wonderful snack that benefits the blood. Literally translated as the fruit of the eye of the dragon, it is beneficial after menstruation and in cases of dizziness. Longan can help with symptoms like insomnia and forgetfulness due to overthinking or overwork. Longan would not be a good idea if you have a cold, infection, or virus. The tonifying power of longan would then feed the pathogenic factor.

Goji berries 枸杞子: These sweet treats also benefit Liver Blood, assisting with blurred vision. Both longan and goji berries are mild enough to be taken regularly for an extended period, benefiting Qi and Blood throughout the body.

Mint 薄荷 tea: Cool and refreshing, these herbs benefit the throat and eyes. They support your body's defensive Qi in the presence of thirst, chills, sensation of warmth, sweat, irritability, red face, and yellow or dry nasal discharge. Mint tea also assists rashes in manifesting and reaching completion.

White chrysanthemum 菊花 tea: White chrysanthemum detoxifies, and mint can address gastrointestinal distress. Wild chrysanthemum 野菊花 can treat itching (a Wood symptom of Wind) when used as an external wash, as well as red eyes with blurred vision. Joel Penner suggests using a pillow filled with wild chrysanthemum for blurry vision.

Raw foods: Fresh produce and sprouted grains invigorate Liver Qi to flow throughout the body. When Liver energy is stagnant, we often find ourselves sighing and feeling blocked. If you feel stuck, try peaches, strawberries, chestnuts, beets, taro root, pine nuts, cherries, broccoli, cauliflower, and cabbage.

Spices: Basil, mustard greens, onions, cardamom, fennel, ginger, rosemary, mint, lemon balm, bay leaf, angelica root, and horseradish can awaken the Wood element.

The healing sound for the Wood element is *Shu*, exhaled after a deep inhale. You may practice this sound meditation with the visualization of green in your Liver, or separately. The sound alone is helpful when stuck in traffic and dealing with irritation at fellow drivers.

Longan fruit is a delicious snack believed to calm the Heart Spirit.

WOOD ACUPRESSURE

Two acupressure points can release tension and unblock Wood Qi. On the top of the foot, you will find Great Rushing 太沖 Tàichōng. One of Ma Dan-yang's Heavenly Star points, it is a location where Qi streams and essential source Qi emerges. The third point on the Liver channel, Great Rushing can address menstrual problems, emotional irritability, headache, and insomnia. Find the crease between your big toe and your second toe, then trace your finger toward your ankle until you feel the junction of your first two metatarsal bones. In the space right before the two bones meet, your Great Rushing point lies. Shoulder Well 肩井 Jiānjǐng is on the Gallbladder channel between the tip of your shoulder bone and the seventh cervical vertebra. Massaging this area can release tension due to anger, preventing Wood Qi from becoming blocked.

The vigorous quality of Wood energy gets things done, and it is this surging inspiration that I hope carries you to the end of this book. As you go forward, remember to balance action with patient reflection. As a Chinese proverb reminds us, pulling up seedlings does not help them grow faster.

CHAPTER 14

HEALING THROUGH COMMUNITY

Relationships heal in the context of power sharing and brave communication. This chapter will support you in weaving yourself back into right relationships through loving communication. A Chinese proverb cautions that both words and water are easy to pour but cannot be recovered once spilled.

Loving communication is often a skillset we must learn. Popular song lyrics, movies, films, and other media model passive aggression, overt aggression, and drama. There is no single correct way to communicate, as different cultures have different norms. But within your cultural context, there are ways to communicate with greater care for yourself and others. It is vital for our species' survival that we develop the skills to navigate complexity with care.

Please note that the suggestions below are intended for relationships characterized by a baseline of mutual respect and earned trust. When dealing with a person whose words are consistently out of sync with their actions, and in the case of any form of abuse (here defined as the act of leveraging power to consistently harm someone with less access to resources), these strategies do not apply. In those conditions, please seek support from survivor-led organizations to get out of the situation.

My evolving practice of loving communication includes:

- Using "I" statements.

- Asking myself, "What is my motive?" before I initiate or engage in communication. This often guides me away from internet arguments with strangers that satisfy a part of me that is arrogant and self-righteous.

- Rehearsing words I need to say in the mirror before I connect with the other person. If needed, I practice with someone I trust.

- Pausing before initiating a challenging conversation to check in with my body and the other person or people about how we're feeling. I try to proceed only if both/all of us are in our window of tolerance.

- Considering scale: What is playing out on the micro level of interpersonal interactions? The meso level of groups and institutions? The macro level of societies at large? What is the appropriate scale of response?

- Considering context: What histories and power dynamics shaped the parties involved over the past several generations?

- Considering timing: What are the parties involved dealing with right now? Is this the best time for this interaction?

- Considering the source: Whose voice is speaking the thoughts that occur to me? Is my first thought something I genuinely believe, or might it reflect the views of my childhood caregivers?

- Reflecting: Naming what I perceive to be occurring and/or reflecting what I heard the other person express, then asking their perspective.

- Boundary-setting: Unapologetically and clearly stating what I need from the other person.

Obviously, these are aspirational practices that I don't embody perfectly. I offer them in hopes that they might be useful to you in striving to treat yourself and others with greater care and intentionality.

CHOSEN FAMILY

The families we are born into don't always have the resources or knowledge we need. Accepting this reality frees up time and energy to co-create relationships that do meet our needs. Beyond our families of origin, we can seek out kindred spirits rather than try to change our birth families. When we meet our relational needs elsewhere, sometimes we discover greater compassion for our relatives as fellow fallible humans. While children cannot choose their households, adults can build intentional communities of care. Not everyone in your blood family may be on the same page, but other beings with similar hearts and cycle-breaker paths will find you.

Family trees may grow rotten or burn, but the Wood element embodies resurrection. After Water element's season of apparent wintery death, Wood is reborn each spring. By growing with your chosen family, you can spread your leaves once more.

CHOSEN FAMILY EXERCISE

1. If you could create a definition of *family* that feels truly supportive, what would it look like? Feel like? Sound like? How would people treat each other? For this exercise, release all notions of what is reasonable or possible.

2. In your definition of *family*, what skills would you and others need to have to support each other at the highest level of care? What support systems would need to be in place? What conditions make liberatory chosen family possible?

3. What steps can you take to increase your capacity to show up for your chosen family with the highest level of care?

4. What people in your life are ready and able to show up and create a chosen family with you? Who has shown in their behavior that they have the capacity to do so?

ACCOUNTABILITY TEAM

Your accountability team consists of people who have the emotional bandwidth to support you in your efforts to break cycles in your lineage. These are people who consent to hold space for you with equal parts rigor and compassion. They may take on and step away from this role based on their own capacity and life circumstances.

In the element Wood, we are preparing to be ancestors who leave this plane with a legacy of action. As you reflect on who can support you in keeping your (manageable, not martyr-like) commitments, consider asking your ancestors for:

- Elders willing and able to guide you

- Peers who share similar values

- A handful of partners who could touch base with you more frequently

If no one comes to mind, that's okay. An affirmation practice can carry you until you cross paths with those who can co-create these kinds of relational containers. Some possible sentence stems:

- I am supported by elders of integrity who show me the way to live a life of deep meaning.

- My peers and I tend our freedom dreams with attention, adaptability, and vision.

- My partnerships are vibrant and spacious enough to hold space for mutually beneficial growth.

If there are people in your life today who might be able to be part of your accountability team, start drafting a request. It may feel odd and vulnerable, which just means you are being brave! Practicing in the mirror can help. Once you've identified your affinity groups, your role, and your learning plan in the following pages, you will have greater clarity on the specific commitments you're asking your accountability team to support you in maintaining. For now, you're feeling out what relationships might be sites where this work can take place in a mutually supportive way.

Each time you bravely reach out, no matter the outcome, please reward yourself for your courage. This can be as simple as making time to stand under a tree and gaze at the leaves dancing in dappled light. As limited humans, we are not in charge of outcomes. To have acted with courage in service of future generations is worthy of honor.

AFFINITY GROUPS AND COALITIONS

Moving out from you in successive layers of intimacy, the chosen family is made up of people who can hold emotional space for you when you need care. The accountability team consists of people who can provide structure, feedback, and encouragement as you work toward greater alignment between your principles and actions. These first two layers are the relational containers that can best hold your personal process.

There is great beauty in belonging amid a diverse assembly with abundant difference: this is the biodiverse, multispecies community we are meant to belong to on Earth. And to belong with our own kind is also sacred. Healing happens across shared experiences and utter difference; all of it is important.

I invite you to start or continue research into local and digital affinity groups organizing around shared values and healing from shared trauma. Make a list of those that appeal to you. Once you've identified affinity groups, research coalitions that are taking action on issues that you care about. These are most likely larger than affinity groups and gather people from many walks of life around shared vision and goals. Save this list as well.

CHAPTER 15

YOUR ACTION PLAN

The elements Metal and Water gave you information about the past: what previous generations and younger versions of your selves did. While we can make moral judgments about those choices, we are living with the effects. Shame and self-punishment do not change the past. When ethical critiques arise, ask yourself how you can shift resources and power now to create different outcomes for the future.

AWARENESS EXERCISE

- Material: What money, property, and assets do you own? Have access to?

- Relational: What connections do you have to people with political power? Wealth? Property? Clout? Assets? Their own connections?

- Cultural: What citizenship papers, language fluency, certificates, and degrees do you possess that grant you access to networks of resources and power?

If taking accountability triggers foundational wounds and you tend to center yourself rather than those impacted, revisit the element Fire. You deserve care and healing for wounds suffered in childhood, but that does not exempt you from accountability when someone else expresses that you have caused harm. Go back to basics: unconditional love for all that you are. Use your self-soothing practices to remind yourself that while you make mistakes, you are not *a* mistake. By tending to your younger selves, you can show up in the present moment and be an agent of healing and integrity.

Before diving into action, assess your capacity and resources. An accurate understanding of what you have at your disposal is essential for Wood element action to be effective. A caring gardener does not overharvest from a fruit tree or trim anything but the branches that have gone dry.

You may take out a piece of paper and draw your name in the center, then write the assets you identified above around your name. Which are easiest to access? Which are farthest away from you? Represent this visually and spatially. Notice how you feel after this exercise. Perhaps go for a walk to activate your sense of agency and metabolize any emotions that arise.

LEARNING PLAN

As future ancestors, we are always learning. We take responsibility for our own growth by continuously listening, reading, and observing.

This is important because we will one day become elders, bewildered by the new terms and ideas of younger generations. The youth need experienced teachers to provide hope, perspective, and guidance. Elders need youth for audacity, energy, and vision.

Your accountability team is a resource to support you with your learning plan. I invite you to take the following steps:

1. Choose an issue to learn about each season.

2. Set specific, measurable, realistic goals for sustainable learning. It's better to do less but do it consistently than take on too much and burn out.

3. Ask someone in your accountability team to help you follow through. A study buddy or reading group might be a win-win!

With a clearer sense of your current sphere of influence, draw upon the wisdom of the element Water to direct your Wood energy. Through conscience-driven action rooted in ancestral experience, you can create a legacy.

ANCESTRAL REDIRECTION EXERCISE

1. As a lineage bearer, what harms from previous generations of your family can you personally work to rectify? What healing can you seed?

2. Whose suffering do you personally benefit from in this lifetime, and how can you work in solidarity with those populations?

3. The answers guide you to the places where you invite you—future ancestor—to focus your time, energy, and resources. It is in sincere ongoing efforts to repair harm that you are directly connected so that you can have the most profound impact on lineage karma.

CONCLUSION

WHAT IS MY ROLE?

None of us can be everything to everyone, just as none of the five energetic phases of Chinese medicine is superior to another. Nature shows us that thriving multispecies communities need many types of beings. There is a niche in the biosphere for myriad forms of life, and there is a role for you.

For us to stay in long-term, mutualistic relationships, we need roles that may stretch us but don't hurt. Human life isn't pure fun, but joy, fulfillment, and pleasure make it possible for us to face the inevitable challenges.

Daoists speak of each person's celestial mandate or "golden road." If those terms feel too religious, perhaps consider "purpose" or "vocation." The Japanese concept of ikigai describes a person's reason for living, a sweet spot between love, skill, and service to the collective.

Sometimes the role we are born to fulfill and the work we are meant to do might not exist yet. What absence, loss, or silence do you feel most acutely? Could your own experience be medicine for us all? You may have been born to write the book you needed to read or record the album you needed to hear. There are people who can only hear the message through you. It is your calling to find them.

Zoom out across space and time, feeling for a vantage point of millennia, and imagine yourself as one small but essential piece of thread in a tapestry woven by countless generations. We do not have infinite time or resources while incarnate in the material plane, so how we spend our energy matters.

Your chosen family and accountability team cradle and carry you as you create your legacy. In your affinity groups and coalitions, you show up in the role best suited for the gifts unique to your strengths and temperament. Your learning plan prepares you to be an elder with wisdom and an open mind. Now, choose your battles.

As you reflect on these questions in this writing exercise, listen to your body and your feelings. What causes or issues bring up dread and irritation? Which fill you with purpose and passion? Which dreams spark a sense of expansiveness in your chest? Which lead to a knot in your stomach? Remember that while a life's work isn't a frivolous diversion, it also won't be sustainable if you physically detest the tasks you take on.

The 28 Daoist constellations encircle the spiritual center, forming the Azure Dragon of the East, the Vermilion Bird of the South, the White Tiger of the West, and the Mysterious Warrior of the North.

STRATEGY EXERCISE

1. What issues affect your life the most directly? Your loved ones? List systems and situations that need to change for you and your communities to thrive.

2. Of the issues that impact you and your communities, which do you feel most passionate about and most capable of organizing for?

3. Have previous generations of your family and/or younger versions of yourself been complicit in harm? If so, what individuals and groups are working to repair that harm?

4. Of the problems that your lineage has contributed to, which do you feel most passionate about and most capable of organizing for?

5. Given the time and money you have available after first meeting your needs and those of your dependents and partner(s), how much can you allocate each week to the causes that are most important to you?

6. With your skills, assets, and temperament, where are you most effective? How can you have the greatest possible impact? In what contexts do you remember feeling your most purposeful? What commonalities do you notice?

7. In which contexts do you feel the least effective, least passionate, and most drained? What commonalities do you notice?

8. How much time and money can you spend each week on causes that are not directly related to your communities and lineage-based amends? This is a discretionary fund of your time and money that you can spend on crises that arise and aid to communities that you are not directly connected to.

9. If you could make a significant impact on one issue, problem, or policy in your lifetime, which would you choose? Why?

10. Imagine that you are looking back at your life from the perspective of a wise elder. What legacy would bring you the the greatest sense of fulfillment? Write, draw, sculpt, or otherwise note what you discover.

Allocate the time and money you have available to the causes you feel most passionate about and effective in supporting. If your financial situation and time commitments shift, take a moment to revisit these questions.

Rainbow Light Visualization

The Five Elements within you mirror the sacred geometry of all creation. I invite you to imagine them as healing energies shining in your being.

Find a comfortable position that allows your spine to unfurl toward the sky. Feel gravity supporting your body at every point of contact with the Earth. With every breath, allow more and more tension drain through your feet. Let your eyelids drop and turn your attention inward to your heart center. You begin to perceive a soft rose glow like that of a candle flame. It shimmers into the form of a phoenix whose wings beat with the drum of your heart.

The rose light flows down to your solar plexus, where it melts into warm gold. A regal dragon with scales of sunlight shines within your center.

The rays of glorious gold reflect back up to your chest, where they soften into the opalescent white of moonlight. As your chest cavity fills with pearl white, you see a snow tiger protecting your heart.

The moonbeams pour down to your pelvis and lower back, deepening into royal blue and ebony. This oceanic luminescence fortifies your lower elixir field and gathers your vitality. A mysterious, dignified tortoise stewards the ancient wisdom of this spiritual center.

The blue brightens to the azure of a clear sky, becoming a waterfall that refreshes your right side body. Below your right rib cage, you feel a vibrant emerald light unfurling with gusto. A jade dragon dances lithe and free.

Suffused with the colors of the rainbow, you feel into your hip bones and ground into your body. As you root down into the center of the earth, you perceive rainbow light coming toward you from the sky: rose light from Mars, golden light from Saturn, white light from Venus, blue light from Mercury, and green light from Jupiter. Let all those colors come together above your crown, merging into one glorious golden light that permeates your being, cleansing and healing you at a genetic level.

Looking up, you see that the stars form the shape of a dragon in the east, a phoenix in the south, a tiger in the west, and a turtle in the north. Right above your head, the North Star shines with the seven stars of the Drinking Gourd. These seven stars descend and alight along the central axis of your body, both your spine and the frontal aspect. Envision the North Star's light gathering at the highest point of your crown and entering your body. Within you, starlight spirals along the DNA in your cell nuclei and mitochondria, restoring your genome to optimum health.

When you feel renewed, gather the light into your crown, then your heart, then below your belly button. Take three deep, slow breaths. Gently wiggle your fingers and toes and open your eyes when you are ready.

The following translation of the Golden Radiance Invocation 金光神咒 calls upon powerful protective light. Repeating it in intervals of three can be calming and restorative.

INVOCATION

Touch your tongue to your soft palate to connect the Sea of Yin and Sea of Yang within you, generating and storing energy through the microcosmic orbit. Breathe into the soles of your feet three times, exhaling with the intention of releasing heaviness. Next, bring your awareness to the center of your chest, breathing three times deeply. From the crown of your head, allow your breath to open you up to celestial support. Now read the following:

> *Mystical ancestors of Earth and Heaven,*
> *Root and source of all that is,*
> *Uncountable lifetimes of cultivation*
> *Prove my true connection with divine oneness.*
> *Throughout the three cosmic spheres,*
> *Surpassing honor upholds the Dao.*
> *My body is one with golden radiance*
> *Permeating and protecting my entire being.*
> *Beyond sight and hearing,*
> *The Dao encircles Earth and Heaven,*
> *Nourishing all lives.*
> *With ten thousand repetitions of this incantation,*
> *My body is one with golden radiance.*
> *Guardians protect the three cosmic spheres.*

Divine protectors of the five directions welcome me.
Ten thousand divinities bow in sacred ceremony
Illuminated by the brilliance of lightning.
Malevolent forces flee the mysterious spirit of thunder.
Primordial wisdom divinely supports me.
The Qi of the Five Elements rises sweetly,
Instantaneously shimmering in golden radiance,
Enveloping and guarding my true essence.
It is so.

This is one of the 八大咒 Eight Great Incantations that Daoists recite in the morning, with ancient potency in the words. Speaking this invocation aloud invites a subtle energetic response from the invisible realms. Afterward, bite your teeth together nine times and swirl the saliva around within your mouth three times. Your cultivation has influenced the water within, which becomes what Daoists call a jade or golden elixir. Swallow this vital medicine with the intention of gathering life force deep in your lower energy center. Take one deep breath with attention below your navel, another around your heart, and the third at the crown of your head.

RADIATE

Like the moon, you are always in the process of waxing and waning. There is no graduation date, no end to your growth, but it is worth it to commemorate the journey. Every full moon is magical. How can you celebrate yourself for the work you have done in this book?

Wherever these words find you, starlight reaches across the space between us. Constellate my brightness with your own, and shine on.

火 土 金 水 木

FURTHER RESOURCES

My hope is that this book is one part of your lineage healing. Transforming your ancestral line is a lifelong process, and there are many powerful tools and teachers along the way.

BOOKS

All About Love: New Visions by bell hooks

The Body Is Not an Apology: The Power of Radical Self-Love by Sonya Renee Taylor

The Body Keeps the Score: Brain, Mind, and Body in the Healing of Trauma by Bessel van der Kolk

body rites: a holistic healing and embodiment workbook for Black survivors of sexual trauma by shena j. young, PsyD

Disability Visibility: First-Person Stories from the Twenty-first Century by Alice Wong

Entering the Tao: Master Ni's Guidance for Self-Cultivation by Hua-Ching Ni

Listen to the Ancestors: Wisdom of Ebomi Cici by Nancy de Souza

Love and Rage: The Path of Liberation through Anger by Lama Rod Owens

Mastering Chi: Strength from Movement by Hua-Ching Ni

My Grandmother's Hands: Racialized Trauma and the Mending of Our Bodies and Hearts by Resmaa Menakem

Osun: Whispering of Wisdom from the Waters by Alisa Orduña, PhD

Ritual: Power, Healing, and Community by Malidoma Patrice Somé

Sister Outsider: Essays and Speeches by Audre Lorde

Undrowned: Black Feminist Lessons from Marine Mammals by Alexis Pauline Gumbs

Workbook for Spiritual Development of All People by Hua-Ching Ni

COURSES

Accountability Mapping
https://accountabilitymapping.thinkific.com

Awaken the Spiritual Wisdoms of Your Ancestors Apprenticeship
https://drvelmalove.clickfunnels.com/optin1664217574263

Become a Good Ancestor
https://www.becomeagoodancestor.com/claim-your-space

Black Feminist Breathing Chorus
https://sangodare.podia.com/breathingchorus

Trauma-Sensitive Mindfulness: The Introductory Guide to Recognizing Trauma, Responding Skillfully, and Preventing Retraumatization
https://davidtreleaven.com/trauma-sensitive-mindfulness-complete/

ORGANIZATIONS

Ancestors in Training
https://ancestorsintraining.org

Black Emotional And Mental Health Collective
https://beam.community

Cheetah House
https://www.cheetahhouse.org

College of Tao
https://www.collegeoftao.org

Ile Orunmila Afedefeyo
https://www.ifaforall.org

International Taoist Meditation Institute
https://www.collegeoftao.org/taoist-meditation.html

The Embodiment Institute
https://www.theembodimentinstitute.org

PODCASTS

Good Ancestor Podcast
   https://laylafsaad.com/good-ancestor-podcast/

Finding Our Way
   https://www.findingourwaypodcast.com

TEACHERS

Initiates of traditional African/Afro-diasporic religions are listed first by their religious name, then by their legal names in parentheses, if they use both publicly.

Ana Laidley

angel Kyodo williams

Awo Falokun Faṣẹgun (Earl White, Jr.)

Awo Fanira Ogunleke Awoyade
   (Hashim Williams)

Cara Kovacs

Colin Bedell

Dana Maman

Daoshing Ni

Ebomi Cici (Nancy de Souza)

Edward Sullivan

Iya Aderonke Adesanya Awoyade

Iya Fayomi Oṣundoyin Egbeyemi
   (Trifari Williams)

Iya Oṣunfunke (Alisa Orduña)

Iya Oṣuntayo Obatolu
   (Felicia Onyi Richards)

Jeffrey C. Yuen

Kahlil Cummings

Lama Rod Owens

Linda Yudin

Luiz Badaró

Maoshing Ni

Mestre Amén Santo

Monica A. Coleman

Olivia Rosewood

Oluwo Falolu Adesanya Awoyade

Oloye Fayomi Falade Aworeni Obafemi

Rachel Hernandez

Robert Hoffman

Rosangela Silvestre

Sanyu Estelle

Shakeinah Davis

Iya Oṣunbunmi Oriṣaṣewa
   (Shena Young)

Velma Love

Vera Passos

Vida Vierra

REFERENCES

Bensky, D., S. Clavey, A. Gamble, E. Stöger, and L. L. Bensky. *Chinese Herbal Medicine: Materia Medica*. Eastland Press, 2004.

Chen, J. K., T. T. Chen, and L. Crampton. *Chinese Medical Herbology and Pharmacology (Vol. 1267)*. Art of Medicine Press, 2004.

Cheng, X., and Y. Wang. *Chinese Acupuncture and Moxibustion*. Foreign Language Press, 2019.

Coyle, D. (1998). "On the Zhenren." In *Wandering at Ease in the Zhuangzi*, edited by R. Ames, 197–210. State University of New York Press, 1998.

Deadman, P., M. Al-Khafaji, and K. Baker. *A Manual of Acupuncture. Journal of Chinese Medicine Publications*, 2016.

"The Eight Great Incantations." Wudang Five Immortals Temple, February 19, 2019, http://fiveimmortals.com/the-eight-great-incantation.

Franks, L. J. *Stone Medicine: A Chinese Medical Guide to Healing with Gems and Minerals*, 1st ed. Healing Arts Press, 2016.

Fruehauf, H. "The Science of Symbols: Exploring a Forgotten Gateway to Chinese Medicine (Part One)." *Journal of Chinese Medicine* 68 (2002): 33–40.

Kaptchuk, T. J. *The Web That Has No Weaver: Understanding Chinese Medicine*. McGraw-Hill, 2008.

Karpman, S. B. *A Game Free Life: The Definitive Book on the Drama Triangle and Compassion Triangle by the Originator and Author. The New Transactional Analysis of Intimacy, Openness, and Happiness*, 1st ed. Drama Triangle Publications, 2014.

Laozi. *The Complete Works of Lao Tzu: Tao Teh Ching and Hua Hu Ching.* Translated by Hua-Ching Ni. Sevenstar Communications, 2013.

Laozi. *Esoteric Tao Teh Ching,* 1st ed. Translated by Hua-Ching Ni. Sevenstar Communications, 2011.

Laozi. *Tao Te Ching: A New English Version.* Translated by Stephen Mitchell. Harper Perennial Modern Classics, 2006.

Maciocia, G. *The Foundations of Chinese Medicine: A Comprehensive Text.* Elsevier, 2015.

Maciocia, G. "Shen and Hun: The Psyche in Chinese Medicine." February 10, 2021. https://giovanni-maciocia.com/shen-and-hun-psyche-in-chinese-medicine.

McCunn, R. L., and K. L. Liu. *Chinese Proverbs.* Chronicle Books, 1991.

Ni, D. *Crane-Style Chi Gong and Its Therapeutic Effects.* Sevenstar Communications, 2015.

Ni, H. *Attune Your Body with Dao-In.* Tao of Wellness Press, 2020.

Ni, H. *8000 Years of Wisdom, Book 1: Conversations with Hua-Ching Ni (Includes Dietary Guidance).* Sevenstar Communications, 2010.

Ni, H. *8000 Years of Wisdom: Volume II: Book 2: Includes Sex and Pregnancy Guidance,* 1st ed. Sevenstar Communications, 1983.

Ni, H. *Entering the Tao: Master Ni's Guidance for Self-Cultivation (1st ed.).* Shambhala, 1997.

Ni, H. *I Ching: The Book of Changes and the Unchanging Truth.* Sevenstar Communications, 1995.

Ni, H. *Tao: The Subtle Universal Law and the Integral Way of Life.* Shrine of the Eternal Breath of Tao, 1979.

Ni, H. *Taoist Inner View of Universe and Immortal Realm.* Sevenstar Communications, 1979.

Ni, H. *Teachings of Chuang Tzu: Attaining Unlimited Life (Wisdom of Three Masters)*. Sevenstar Communications, 2009.

Ni, H. *Workbook for Spiritual Development of All People*. Shrine of the Eternal Breath of Tao, 1984.

Ni, H., D. Ni, and M. Ni. *Strength from Movement: Mastering Chi*. Tao of Wellness Press, 2009.

Ni, M. *Live Your Ultimate Life*. Sevenstar Communications, 2016.

Ni, M. *The Tao of Nutrition*, 3rd ed. Sevenstar Communications, 2009.

Ni, M., and H. Ni. *The Eight Treasures Energy Enhancement Exercise*. Sevenstar Communications, 1996.

Ni, M. S. *Live Long, Live Strong: An Integrative Approach to Cancer Care and Prevention*. Tao of Wellness Press, 2022.

Paynter, J. M., and J. D. Schaefer. *Daoist Morning and Evening Altar Recitations*. Parting Clouds Daoist Press, 2019.

Penner, J. "Herb Index—Chinese Herbs." American Dragon. Last updated 2017. https://www.americandragon.com/IndividualHerbsIndex2.html.

Pitchford, P. *Healing with Whole Foods: Asian Traditions and Modern Nutrition*, 3rd rev. ed. North Atlantic Books, 2002.

Zhuangzi. *Zhuangzi: The Complete Writings*. Translated by Brook Ziporyn. Hackett Publishing Company, 2020.

ENDNOTES

INTRODUCTION

2   "At all scales of human comprehension . . .": As with the capitalized names of organs, Blood in this context is not equivalent to the biomedical definition. You can think about Blood in Chinese medicine as the literal fluid that carries hemoglobin and erythrocytes, but it also carries specific meaning and interpretation within a Chinese medical interpretive schema.

7   "Audre Lorde wrote . . .": A. Lorde. *Uses of the Erotic: The Erotic as Power.* Tucson, AZ: Kore Press, 2000.

10   "Robert Hoffman explains Qi as . . .": R. Hoffman. "Week 1—Foundations." *CM111 Principles and Theories I.* Lecture presented at the Principles and Theories of Chinese Medicine, September 3, 2019.

10   "Hua-Ching Ni calls the 'universal energy net.'": H. Ni. *Tao: The Subtle Universal Law and the Integral Way of Life.* Santa Monica, CA: Sevenstar Communications, 1995.

14   "According to the teachings of Jeffrey C. Yuen . . .": L. J. Franks. *Stone Medicine: A Chinese Medical Guide to Healing with Gems and Minerals.* Rochester, VT: Healing Arts Press, 2016.

16   "The Heart Spirit gives us . . .": I specify the spirit of the Heart when referring to the Five Spirits because spirit has multiple meanings in different contexts of Daoism and Chinese medicine.

19   "Instead of comparing my external appearance . . .": S. A. Tate and K. Fink, "Skin Colour Politics and the White Beauty Standard," in *Beauty and the Norm*, ed. Claudia Liebelt, Sarah Böllinger, and Ulf Vierke (Palgrave Macmillan, 2019), 283–97.

21   "Audre Lorde taught . . .": A. Lorde. *Our Dead Behind Us: Poems*.
      New York, NY: W. W. Norton, 1994.

21   "Problems arise when we refuse to 'follow the rightness . . .'" Zhuangzi.
      Zhuangzi: The Complete Writings. Translated by Brook Ziporyn.
      Hackett Publishing Company, 2020.

CHAPTER 1

27   "Self-soothing helps our bodies manage distress . . .": V. Ellison, "The 'Window
      of Tolerance': A Tool for Self-Regulation," Columbia Theological Seminary,
      https://www.ctsnet.edu/the-window-of-tolerance-a-tool-for-self-regulation.

27   "This model of understanding emotion regulation . . .": D. J. Siegel. *The
      Developing Mind: How Relationships and the Brain Interact to Shape Who
      We Are*. New York: Guilford Press, 2012.

28   "The scientific community has identified biomedical benefits . . .": J. Yim,
      "Therapeutic Benefits of Laughter in Mental Health: A Theoretical Review,"
      Tohoku Journal of Experimental Medicine, 239, no. 3 (2016): 243–49.

28   "Effie Chow, a world-renowned energy healer and humanitarian, recommends
      . . .": R. W. Perez. *Discoveries in Alternative Medicine. American Health Journal*.
      PBS, 2009.

31   "Inner Pass 內關 treats chest and Heart issues . . .": Western is an imperfect
      term for biomedicine that I use here simply to be clear that acupuncture and
      herbalism should not be your first and only treatment for cardiovascular
      issues. The idea of East versus West is a construct of Orientalism.

CHAPTER 2

38   "A beautiful introduction to June Jordan's assertion . . .": A. P. Gumbs,
      "June Jordan Solves the Energy Crisis: Love Is Lifeforce," Feminist Wire,
      March 23, 2016, https://thefeministwire.com/2016/03/june-jordan-solves
      -the-energy-crisis-love-is-lifeforce.

CHAPTER 3

44   "Because our bodies remember violations . . .": "Adverse Childhood Experiences (ACEs)," National Center for Injury Prevention and Control, Division of Violence Prevention, Centers for Disease Control and Prevention, April 2, 2021, https://www.cdc.gov/violenceprevention /aces/index.html.

44   "Internal family systems theory is a framework . . .": "About Us," Internal Family Systems Institute, https://ifs-institute.com/about-us.

44   "Relational experiences in the first several years of life . . .": R. M. Sullivan, "The Neurobiology of Attachment to Nurturing and Abusive Caregivers," *Hastings Law Journal* 63, no. 6 (2012): 1553–70.

CHAPTER 4

52   "Nurturing life 養生 is an ancient Daoist practice . . .": "Yang Sheng—the Ancient Chinese Approach to Self-Care," Wu Wei Wisdom, April 27, 2019, https://www.wuweiwisdom.com/yang-sheng.

54   "As one of the most-researched acupuncture points . . .": X. You et al., "Zusanli (ST36) Acupoint Injection with Neostigmine for Paralytic Postoperative Ileus following Radical Gastrectomy for Gastric Cancer: A Randomized Clinical Trial," *Journal of Cancer* 9, no. 13 (2018): 2266–74, https://doi.org/10.7150/jca.24767.

CHAPTER 5

65   "Catherine Kerr cautions against jumping to conclusions . . .": L. Heuman. "Don't Believe the Hype," *Tricycle: The Buddhist Review*, October 1, 2014.

65   "Cheetah House is a nonprofit . . .": https://www.cheetahhouse.org /cheetah-house-resources.

65   "Reading Audre Lorde's *Uses of the Erotic* . . .": A. Lorde. *Uses of the Erotic: The Erotic as Power*. Tucson, AZ: Kore Press, 2000.

CHAPTER 7

82   "Wearing white cloth and golden jewelry . . .": White is a color of mourning in many Asian cultures, so be mindful of all-white attire if you're invited to an Asian celebration.

CHAPTER 10

117   "For example, a well-established Haudenosaunee philosophy . . .": G. Morris, "For the Next Seven Generations: Indigenous Americans and Communalism," in *Communities Directory: A Guide to Cooperative Living* (Fellowship for Intentional Community, 1995).

118   "Take some time to ask relatives . . .": One cruel legacy of racial slavery is that specific information about ancestral roots on the African continent can be difficult to find. Painful truths of all kinds can come to the surface. Please be gentle with yourself during this process.

118   "Priestess-in-training Omiṣeye Williams says . . .": O. Williams. "Feeding Ancestors." Los Angeles, July 7, 2020.

119   "Ethically sourced fragrances . . .": White sage or *Salvia apiana* is holy to Indigenous peoples and is a keystone species in its ecosystem. I strongly discourage purchasing and using this plant for smudging if you are not an indigenous person whose ancestors have traditionally practiced with it.

122   "The Water element relates to the depths of the collective unconscious . . .": Many thanks to Dreamscapes Academy for deepening my dreamwork practice. Sanyu Estelle, Tara Burke, Kris Adams, and my fellow academy members are an inspiration.

124   "Edward Sullivan suggests envisioning the seven stars . . .": E. Sullivan. Lecture. *InfiniChi 2a*. Presented at the InfiniChi 2a, May 18, 2020.

CHAPTER 11

129 "Intentional deep breathing is associated with reduced symptoms . . .": A. Zaccaro et al., "How Breath-Control Can Change Your Life: A Systematic Review on Psycho-Physiological Correlates of Slow Breathing," *Frontiers in Human Neuroscience* 12 (2018): 353, https://pubmed.ncbi.nlm. nih.gov/30245619/.

130 "James Baldwin wrote, 'Not everything that is faced can be changed . . .'": J. Baldwin. "As Much Truth as One Can Bear; To Speak Out About the World as It Is, Says James Baldwin, Is the Writer's Job as Much of the Truth as One Can Bear." *The New York Times*, January 14, 1962, sec. T.

133 "Baba Falokun Faṣegun, priest of Ifá, says . . .": E. White. "IFÁ." *Ile Orunmila Afedefeyo Beach Service.* Lecture presented at the Ile Orunmila Afedefeyo Beach Service, May 21, 2017.

134 "Priestess Iya Fayomi Oṣundoyin Egbeyemi says . . .": Egbeyemi et al. "A Talk on Ancestors and Ancestral Practices in These Times." *Sonyi's Salon.* July 29, 2020.

CHAPTER 13

153 "The character for the Ethereal Soul . . .": This does not necessarily refer to a negative entity that haunts living beings. The character 鬼 can be a nonliving consciousness with neutral connotations.

INDEX

IMAGE CREDITS

ACKNOWLEDGMENTS

This book is fruit from my branches, and it wouldn't exist without the soil that nourishes my roots. The land that has supported me since birth is home to Indigenous peoples, and as a settler, the least I can do is acknowledge their sovereignty. I have occupied the homelands of Kumeyaay, Occaneechi-Saponi, Tuscarora, Tongva, Wampanoag, Narragansett, Chumash, Paraguaçu, Caeté, Tupinambá, and Temiminó nations. I returned part of my advance to Tongva people and the Indigenous Mental Health Awareness Network International as a practice of reciprocity.

I give thanks to Colin Bedell and Kate Zimmermann for their belief in me as a writer, and Cara Kovacs for hosting the space where I met Colin. With Shakeinah Davis, Colin and Cara incubated my nascent potential as a spiritual teacher.

Grandma Suchin Lin Lee published her memoir and showed me that our stories matter. My mother, an accomplished author, nurtured my love of reading and taught me how to write. These generations of women faced obstacles they don't speak about, and I honor them for the sacrifices they made to give me life.

So many Asian people have generously and patiently taught me about my heritage. My father, William Tsung-Liang Lee, taught me Yang style taiji-quan and imparted the cultural priorities of our lineage. His humility, dedication, and inner strength put food on my table and inspire me daily. My Lee and Lin relatives are endlessly patient with my diasporic questions and the language barrier between us, especially Melissa, who translates for us.

Sunhay You has believed in me as a writer since we were teenagers, and our friendship is a gift. Thien Hau Temple 天后宫 Chùa Bà Thiên Hâu is my heart's home, and the elders of the Camau Association show me what is possible when a community works together in service of something greater. API-Equality Los Angeles showed me that gender-diverse Asian people can find belonging and organize in solidarity with oppressed peoples. Millennia of generations of the Ni family have protected and preserved Daoist and Chinese medical knowledge, and OmNi (also known as Hua-Ching Ni) generously shares this inheritance. His sons, Dr. Daoshing Ni and Dr. Mao-shing Ni, continue this legacy through their books, teaching, the College of Tao, and Yo San University of Traditional Chinese Medicine. I am one of many beneficiaries of the Ni family's service to humanity, as a student at these schools.

As I traced the transatlantic connections to my maternal ancestors, Linda McDermott and Brendan Curran opened doors with fierce compassion. In Éireann, great-uncle Antóin Mac Gabhann and his family have welcomed my diasporic line with extraordinary generosity. Making Daoist offerings in great-aunt Debbie McDermott's backyard in central Ireland was a moment of ancestral magic for which I thank my parents and all my relations.

My loved ones' support allowed me the freedom to create this text. Augusto Ícaro is my fountain of encouragement, patience, humor, and sweetness. Ben and Annie's cabin was a sanctuary. Dona Célia and Tia Silvania's homes gave me shelter as this book came into being, and Dom José Augusto's motorcycle took us where we needed to go. Auntie Linda, Sam and Kir, Uncle Bob, Daniel, Julia Rose, and my sister Isabelle Dao-Ahn show up for me with unconditional love. The Vaughan family, Jeanne, Brendan, and Reverend Kathy help this Sagittarius stay grounded as I seek the heavens.

My spiritual teachers leave footprints I follow toward good character. Baba Falokun Faṣẹgun, Iya Fayomi Oṣundoyin Egbeyemi, and Dona Cici embody courage, compassion, and integrity. Studying their words and following their guidance has brought me out of misery into a life I didn't believe I deserved. Baba and Iya's congregation, Ile Orunmila Afedefeyo, has given me the blessing of belonging. I give thanks to Oluwo Falolu Adesanya Awoyade, Iya Aderonke Adesanya Awoyade, and all the elders of their lineage in Ode Remo and Ibadan. May the spirit of Late High Chief Eniolorunda Adesanya Awoyade rest in majesty and watch over them. I pay respects to Iya Bezita de Oxum, Babalorixá Bira de Sango, Babalorixá Rychelmy, and all the members of Ilê Axé Opó Afonjá, Ilê Axé Opô Aganju, and Ilê Asé Ojisé Olodumare. It will take many lifetimes to express the depths of my gratitude.

ABOUT THE AUTHOR

李道玲 Camellia Lee [they/she] is a Qigong and meditation teacher, artist, ancestral guide, energy healer, community organizer, and freelance writer/editor.

Camellia is the firstborn of the firstborn of the eldest son in the 李 Lee clan. The past three generations of their paternal lineage studied Western biomedicine, but family stories say that an earlier ancestor was a traditional village healer. In 2011, a spiritual journey in rural Taiwan led Camellia to a temple of Mazu 媽祖婆, beginning more than a decade of devotion to this goddess, including participation in the holy 白沙屯媽祖進香 pilgrimage in 2017. Camellia's practice of Chinese folk religion honors the historical syncretism between Buddhism, Daoism, and indigenous Chinese animism.

Camellia studies at Yo San University of Traditional Chinese Medicine, the College of Tao, and the International Taoist Meditation Institute. They are a member of the American Society of Acupuncturists Student Committee and a certified Self-Healing Qigong instructor sanctioned to practice InfiniChi® energy healing in the Ni tradition. Other forms Camellia has studied include Eight Treasures Qigong, Chen Style Taijiquan Sword Form, Dao-In Qigong, Harmony Tai Chi, Qigong for Weight Management, Crane-Style Qigong, and Qigong Meditations for Cancer Treatment and Prevention.

In November 2022, Camellia was initiated into the sacred mysteries of Òṣun and Obatalá in the lineage of Oluwo Falolu Adesanya Awoyade in Ode Remo, Nigeria. For more than a decade, they have studied under Babalawo Falokun Ogunkeye Faṣegun and Iya Fayomi Oṣundoyin Egbeyemi in the spiritual house Ile Orunmila Afedefeyo.